"Game Crazy:

Part One – Generations"

Tyrome Lee, Jr.

Post Script Publishing

© 2017 Post Script Publishing. All rights reserved.
ISBN 978-0-578-19774-6

To the person who has always shown me love no matter the circumstance. In your pursuit to make a way for me, you disregarded morals and became ignorant to what was right or wrong. You shielded me the best way you could, and did whatever you had to do to make sure I never went without. I have had really good friends who deceived me and let me down, family members who broke my heart and wished the worst on me; but you were always my refuge. I appreciate you. Even in your own darkest times, you never deprived me of anything. I love everything and everyone that went into making you, and everything made from you. You are my first friend, my queen, and I will always be loyal to you. I love you, Ms. Debra Renee Chocklon...

-Ty

Preface

We look at our lives and the circumstances we come across, and develop the absolute truth of our existence. Our neighborhood, families, friends, and those that we come across are the main benefactors of what we believe our truths to be. We learn that our truths are evaluated by others as we evaluate those who are unfamiliar to our way of living. As human beings, we are predisposed to making decisions that are not intended to bring us out of despair; rather, we make decisions to help alleviate our disparities and simply make them more manageable. We embody every aspect of the hood as a means to an end. We glorify the systematically biased living conditions as we take advantage of our disproportionate distribution of wealth. We ignore the fact that others have profited from the trauma we have endured for generations. Throughout history, we've witnessed the discriminatory actions taken against our people since post-slavery. From the Jim Crow laws, denial of rights, redlining, which leads us to the Prison Industrial Complex, the odds have been stacked against us. Now, we have been educated enough to know who our enemies are, how they work, and what methods they use the keep us in a distained state. We have formulated many plans of action that it may take for us to rise as a people, but fail to realize the rules of positioning. Jamaican political leader and proponent of the Pan-Africanism Movement, Marcus Garvey, warned us about the psychological impact of belonging to the oppressed class, and the main methods and weapons used by our oppressors. Garvey quoted, "When oppressing people, the main goal is to make them the main mechanism and component of their own oppression." With that being said, are we prolonging our own oppression by becoming our own weapons of despair?

Introduction

This book is based on my life events and the atrocities that I have witnessed over a 30-year time span. Follow me as I go from a project kid, to disobedient adolescent, to a small-time drug dealer, and a full-fledged gangster over a span of a couple of decades. I describe my multiple run-ins with law enforcement and the many losses that I took while trying to progress in Seattle's street life. I share events and stories that include close friends, family members, associates, and adversaries that I have encountered. I am inviting you into my world, as I have perceived it. I describe the psychological, physiological, and sociological impact that my environment had on me, and those closest to me. Most of you who know me, now, have no idea what I've been through, my pains, trials, or tribulations. I changed many names, circumstances, and even the chronological time of certain events to protect the guilty; most importantly, because some of these crimes are still open cases. Choosing to assimilate into society and embrace the status quo, severely limited my options. This caused me to adapt to my environment by menacing and defying the cultural norms of my community. Nobody who is confined within a system can progress without creating an unstable mindset to fit the criteria of their confinement. This mindset is crazy. We call the system "The Game" because you have to know how to play it for what it's worth. You have to be crazy to think that you can outplay this game. Therefore, we become Game Crazy…

"I tell you what. Show me a man who hasn't made a bunch of mistakes, and I'll show you a man who hasn't made enough decisions. Our predisposition to taking these necessary chances is genetically installed in our genes, which are activated from the moment of birth. The act of failing is not necessarily genetically passed down, but our failures are comprised of behaviors that can cause an entire community to be doomed to failure. Our failures are definite, but not predictable. We all fail. Some fail more often than others and some fail on a larger magnitude."

Where the Game Comes From

"Check this out, Son. The rules to this game are so skewed that only a true fool would follow them. You'd be alright if you did so, but you'd only have minimal success. The only way to be a boss is if you make your own rules while respecting the ethics of the game's blueprint. There's gonna be plenty of times you'll have to go against the grain; but your style of hustling will make others respect you. No one has ever made it to the top of this game by following the rules step-by-step. You have to step outside of your comfort zone in order to progress. The ones that do follow the rules do nothing more but demonstrate compliance to another man's game and make good soldiers, at best. As bosses, we progress by making new rules, and amending the old ones as we move up and the times change. In order to be respected, you gotta reach heights that others have never witnessed. Both suckas and real hustlers love a trendsetter! Even if they despise the person, they'll still have to respect the hustle. One of the most important things you have to realize is that this is a dirty game; and it's being played by some dirty players. Trust will get you killed. You have to be loyal to yourself before you display loyalty to anyone or anything else." I honestly had no idea what this guy was talking about, but for some reason it made all the sense in the world. I've always thought that people who thought outside the box would always suffer the consequences of not being a part of success and progression. Sure, there were a few exceptions. But who's going to take that chance when the odds are horrifically stacked against them? My mom always said that my dad was somewhat of a genius. But I never understood how this kind of genius always ended up in prison? When I asked her, she said, "Your dad's only problem is his flamboyance and the complete absence of common sense." I thought, "Figures." I mean, how does a guy with no job and no reasonable source of income, afford to get the whole front grill of his Cadillac dipped in gold? My dad was tall, dark, and had jerry curl that hung all the way down to the middle of his back. He walked around in designer clothes and was draped in jewelry. He was totally clueless to the amount of heat he was attracting. One time, I heard my Grandma Johnnie say, "Look at Tyrome running around looking like Black Jesus, selling crack up and down Union like its legal!" But hey, if you got people you trust working for you, handling all the business, and all you got to do is collect the money and orchestrate deals; it'll be impossible for the fuzz to bring up charges on you. You ever heard of RICO?

    I remember when my dad popped up at our house in the spring of 1993. Three years earlier, he was sentenced to 15 years in federal prison. I was now approaching my 8th grade graduation. My brother and I spazzed out when we saw him pull up and hop out of our Uncle Mikey's car. We couldn't believe he was out! He looked the same as he did the last time we saw him. It was like the sun finally shining during hard times. The last time my dad was out was in 1990; he balled out of control. He made himself a millionaire in less than two years from slanging dope. He had money to the ceiling and he treated us like little kings! He and my mom separated while he was doing his first prison stretch in 1984. She met Craig and had another baby shortly, thereafter. When my dad got out there was no love lost between them. As a matter of fact, Craig and him were cool and even did some business together.

My dad ended up marrying this fine ass gold digging chick named Jackie in 1989, and they had a baby girl together. They had a penthouse that looked like a palace. Yeah, he had it all: He had money, women, cars, and haters. I said haters because people were always trying to scheme up a plan to knock him off. He was even shot on a couple of occasions but it never resulted in anything critical, because he always had a good exit strategy. Dad stood about six-feet tall, had a slender build, and was a better runner than he was a fighter. He got shot in the leg on one occasion, and in his backside on another. His retaliation game was strong because he kept killers on the payroll. Dad always said, "With money you can buy power." So, he bought a few loyal soldiers to do his dirty work.

The Feds came for him in 1990. They hit him hard and tried to take the whole family down with him. He ended up taking a plea so they wouldn't prosecute his momma and sister. This is why I didn't understand why he was out. I didn't care though. I just knew that things were going to be good because he was home. Dad loved Tyree and I, equally. However, he spent more time with me because I was older, and we had deeper conversations than the ones he had with my brother. He spent more time with me because he was "schooling me" around this time. I was Tyrome Lee, Jr. and I looked just like the man. Sometimes, I'd be out in public and people would just walk up to me and say, "Hey, aren't you a Lee?" I'd say, "Yeah, why?" They would reply, "Because you look just like them. Which one are you?" When I told them who I was they would start telling me how much of a real dude my dad was, and how they used to do this and that, or how good of friends they were. This was a constant occurrence in my life growing up. Being Tyrome, Jr. even helped me get out of a few sticky situations.

"Bullshit ain't nothing. I'll put a stamp on this game one way or another. I'll either display phenomenal hustling to get it by any means necessary, or I'll plant the seeds and make sure my bloodline lives forever! The truth of the matter is that I'm extraordinary; I set trends, break rules, defy odds and accept all challenges. I'll pass all of these good qualities down to my offspring. The only problem is that they'll also inherit my shortcomings."

Predisposition

1981 - 1982

As far back as I can remember…my dad had always been in jail. There were only a few times I can remember him being out in my younger days, but it wasn't for very long. My earliest memories of my dad were when we stayed in Lakeshore Village, in the south end of Seattle. This was maybe 1981 -

1982? We had a little two-bedroom apartment. It was just my mom, dad, and I living there. I was two or three years old. My mom was 20 years old and my dad was about 18. I remember there being hella boxes and packaged merchandise in our house. There would be boxes of unopened electronics and shit. Dad always had some kind of hustle brewing. He had a bunch of cars outside of our apartment and some up at his mom's house. If he wasn't robbin and stealin, then he was wheelin and dealin. He was a bonafide hustler! If he didn't have it, he could get it. If he couldn't get, then they didn't have it. He tried to do a little pimping, but my mom wasn't having it. I remember her waking up in the morning and finding hoes sleeping in her living room. She'd wake them up and start kicking them out of the house. Dad would say, "Baby, let them rest. They've been working all night making me some money." She would reply, "Well, take them bitches home to sleep! You do whatever you want in the streets, Tyrome. Just don't bring that shit home with you; including hoes!"

The Lakeshore Village had one entrance. So, there was only one way in, and one way out. At the beginning of the month, the mailman came to deliver welfare checks and food stamps. Of course, he started at the entrance. My Dad and his cousin would be waiting for him by the entrance and rob his ass. They were only able to do this a couple of times a year, because once he got robbed, he'd be back with police protection for the next few months. Once the authorities figured that the coast was clear and that it was a random event, they'd pull it off again.

My mom and dad met at Garfield High School, in the Central District (CD). My mom's name was Debbie. She was considered as one of the "good girls" and my dad was considered as a "hood". She was a junior and my dad was a freshman. When he got to high school, everyone already knew who he was or had heard about him. He was always involved in something and spent a lot of time in juvenile detention due to his numerous run-ins with the law as a teenager. He would always get sentenced to weekend lock-up. That's when they would let you go home Monday through Friday to attend school and be with your family, but you would have to turn yourself in to juvenile hall for the weekends. That meant he did most of his dirt during the week.

My dad had one older brother, Jerome, who had a knack for automobiles. He was also well known but lacked the charismatic personality of my dad. He had two younger brothers named Shelton and Tommy, and a baby sister, Vernice. His momma, Grandma Maureen, was sort of the brains of the family. She was family oriented, which could be attributed to her Caribbean roots, and she manifested the art of manipulation. She was also good with money. This was strange to me because I remember her telling me that she dropped out of school in the 8th grade to work and help her parents support her other siblings. This is where my dad got most of his game from. His dad, my grandpa, Jerome Sr., was a straight up madman. I mean...he was caring, loving, and supported his family. But he definitely wasn't the one to cross! This man had been to hell and back. He was a Jamaican immigrant who, at the age of 13, came to America by himself after a dispute with his own father. He lived on the streets for years before stabilizing himself with a job, house, and a family. However, Grandpa had a drug problem. He hung out with a motorcycle gang that did heavy drugs in the 70's and 80's. He once robbed a bank and tried to get off with an insanity plea. The courts weren't going for it. This pissed my grandpa off and he attempted to escape by setting fire to the jail. It was a failed attempt but the courts recognized that only a madman would try something so daring and destructive. He got off and spent 6 months in Western State Mental Institution before being released. Grandpa worked as a trucker. He would be gone for weeks at a time driving semi-trucks across the country. When he came home, he'd pay all the bills, rest, spend time with the family, and then he would disappear for days with his biker buddies. Often times, Grandma would find herself driving around town looking for him with a station wagon full of kids.

Once my dad got older, he started doing his own thing and was getting into trouble with the law. It really pissed my grandpa off. He and Grandma would always have to go pick him up from the juvenile detention center or the local precinct when he was a teenager. My dad would constantly test my grandpa and try to defy him. The end result would always be my dad getting his ass kicked. As my dad got older, things escalated between him and his dad as he continued to define his own manhood. When my dad realized he couldn't beat his dad physically, weapons started being used against one another. My dad fired the first shot. These niggas actually went to war with each other on numerous occasions. My dad always took it there. To this day, I still believe my dad has to be the only person in history to ever do a drive-by on his own parent's house. After that incident, it wasn't safe for my dad to even go to his own home. One day my grandpa busted into our house, with his shotgun in tow, looking for my dad. After doing a destructive search of our two-bedroom apartment, he pointed the gun at my mom and said, "Wer dat lil nigga be?!"

My mom almost shit on herself! She said, "I don't know! I don't know!" He said, "Well wen ya see heem, tell em he cont hide fer too long!" He gave me a kiss on my forehead and left. The only way the beef would die down is when my dad would stay gone long enough for Grandpa to forget or after Grandpa was coming down from one of his binges. Dad would send his brother Jerome over there to see where Grandpa's head was at. Grandpa and Jerome were close. If Jerome said that the coast was clear, my dad would call the house and ask for a truce with his dad. This type of shit would happen every 6 months or whenever my dad thought his balls were bigger than his dad's.

My mom and dad both came from the same side of the tracks; just different trains. Debbie's mom, my grandma Johnnie Mae, married young but divorced when things weren't working out. She had two daughters from two past marriages. My mom had one younger sister, my aunt, Lisa. My grandma raised her children on her own and went to night school. Big Momma, my great-grandma, would watch my mom and aunt while Grandma Johnnie attended night school. Eventually, she got her PhD in psychology and opened up her own private practice. Primarily, she raised my mom and aunt in Seattle's Central District (CD). Grandma Johnnie worked crazy hours and attended church faithfully. She wasn't much of a disciplinarian, but she didn't take much shit either! She had a bunch of brothers and sisters that didn't amount to much, but she never thought anything less of them or put herself up on a pedestal. In fact, Grandma Johnnie Mae was very down to earth and had a very good sense of humor.

I loved riding the bus as a youngster. No...actually, they fascinated me. I don't know why? I had all of the bus schedules and knew all of the bus numbers and routes. As a matter of fact, I taught myself how to read by reading bus schedules. If anyone wanted to know what bus went where, I knew. I knew what time they arrived and what time they would get you to your destination. My momma thought something was wrong with me. She believed that I was autistic or something. Her mom, my Grandma Johnnie, was a psychologist. She knew that nothing was wrong with me. She would say, "Ain't nothing wrong with that baby. He's just smart. Shit, he might grow up and be something." Grandma Johnnie figured I was "geographically" gifted. I would sit in the front of the bus and ask the bus driver all sorts of questions. It was like a three-year-old performing a job review. I wanted to know how far the buses travelled and how far the bus numbers counted upward. I would ask questions like, "Why are the routes and numbers of the buses scrambled around" and "Why don't some of the buses run on weekends"? I even gave my suggestions on routes that needed to be included and changes that needed to be made. They always got a kick out of me. I'm pretty sure that I was the topic of discussion at the local bus station every once in a while.

My dad had a patna named Ricki C. He was one of his robbing buddies. My dad only hung out with him to plan or commit robberies; they had nothing else in common. My dad liked performing jobs with him because of the way he stayed calm under pressure. Dad knew that Ricki was a killer. In fact, it was rumored that when Ricki was 14-years-old, he killed his uncle because he heard that he molested his younger sister. He denied doing this, but remained the only suspect in the case. However, charges were never brought up and eventually the heat on him died down. He was implicated in a couple of other incidents but was never charged in any of those cases either.

It was spring of 1982. I was three-years-old and my mom was pregnant with my younger brother, Tyree. We were on the bus headed to an appointment because my mom was upset at my dad for not coming home for three days. She kicked him out, made him move all of his shit out of the house, and refused to accept anything from him. On this particular day, mom and I were already on the bus when Ricki got on. He was drunk and extremely talkative that day. He started up a conversation with my mom, which surprised her because he wasn't much of a talker. The conversation went south when he started bad mouthing about my dad to her. He revealed that he once had feelings for my mom and how he could treat her way better than my dad. My mom was weirded out by him and moved seats. Consequently, this made him mad, so he followed her and became verbally abusive. She told him, "Ricki, you know you're gonna be in for it when Tyrome finds out about this!" He said, "Fuck that nigga, Tyrome! He knows where I be!" We got off the bus.

Later, my mom met up with my dad to tell him about how Ricki was trippin on the bus. Dad was fumed but confused at the same time. He didn't fear Ricky, but he knew confronting him wouldn't be easy. He knew that Ricky was a killer and didn't have any morals. The only conversations that they ever had were about business. He didn't know who this guy was outside of that. So, my dad turned to the one guy who he thought knew crazy…his father. Grandpa didn't sit down long enough to hear the entire story.

When my dad told him about a guy talking crazy to me and my mom on the bus, it was go time. He simply said three words: "Where he at?" Grandpa didn't play when it came to someone fucking with his children or grandchildren. The word was that he nearly killed a man a few years back for putting hands on my Uncle Tommy. My dad was pissed about the current situation and didn't want to address it sober. He grabbed a fifth of Brandy and some valium to knock the nervous edge off. He wasn't nervous about confronting Ricki. He was more nervous about confronting Ricki with his dad. Sure, he thought Ricki was crazy. But he *KNEW* his dad was nuts. He was the only man he knew to have a bar fight with himself.

My dad found out that Ricki and his patnas were at Othello Park. When they got close, they turned off their lights, hopped out, and walked up quietly. When they reached the crowd with shotguns in hand, everyone ran except Ricki. He was still drunk, yet, surprised. Ricki knew that my dad wasn't a violent man. That may have been why he came at my mother the way he did; because he didn't expect much retaliation. Ricki asked, "Whachu want, Tyrome? And who's this old nigga you with?" Grandpa raised the shotgun to Ricki's head and cocked it back one time. Ricki didn't flinch. He wasn't scared a bit. He said, "Don't waste your time trying to scare me with your guns. Handle your business or let me go on about mine." Grandpa knew exactly what kind of crazy this was, and killing him wouldn't have done any justice in the matter. He thought they'd actually be doing this guy a favor if they killed him. Emasculating him would send a better message. Grandpa said, "Ok, batty mon'. I comprehen ya…Say Tyrome, blow dis nigga's balls off!" Ricki bitched up

real quick and went straight into apologetic mode. He
pleaded with and begged my dad to not shoot, but
this just pissed my grandpa off. He pointed the
shotgun to Ricki's head again and said, "Tyrome, if
you don't shoot dis bumbaclot's, I'm gonna retire
him ma self. I'm growin tired of da whining!" My
dad shot him and ran back to the car. Grandpa walked
and took his time doing so.

 The police came to our house the next morning.
It was Detective Randall and a couple of blue and
whites. Randall and my dad had history. He'd been
chasing after him for years. He arrested my dad
numerous times as a juvenile and an adult. Randall
knew whenever there was some kind robbery, heist,
or stick-up, my dad was either involved or knew
something about it. He didn't like my dad because he
never talked or gave anybody up. When he did talk,
he led him in the wrong direction. One time, he gave
Randall some information about a robbery that led to
him doing a drug raid on a Jewish synagogue! He
kicked my dad's ass for that and broke his nose, and
told his Captain that my dad eluded and swung first.
But on this particular morning, he was looking for
him regarding an attempted murder. Randall told my
mom that they knew everything about the incident
because Ricki was cooperating. They said if she
didn't help bring him in, she was going to be brought
up on co-conspiracy charges for motivating my dad
to shoot Ricki. She didn't budge. She knew it was a
bluff tactic.

 The police had a tougher time when they went to
apprehend my grandpa. He was home and refused to
go without a fight! He claimed to not know what they
were talking about, denied being at the scene, and
refused to let them search the house. After a violent
scuffle, they eventually subdued him and took him in.

My dad was on the run. He would move from house to house and lay up with different women every other night. My mother and I barely saw him because he thought that we were being surveillanced. They charged my grandpa with assault but had no evidence. Ricki was pissed off. He wanted to retaliate but couldn't figure out how. Doctors said that he would make a full recovery with some reconstructive surgery, but he would never be able to reproduce. He thought about doing something to me or my mom, but knew that the cops would be all over him if he did. He was drunk when he got shot and couldn't fully remember what my grandpa looked like. He fucked up on the line-up, which led to my grandpa getting a reasonable bail amount and being let back onto the streets. Ricki figured that the best way to retaliate was to tell the police who shot him. He knew the cops had been after my dad for some time now, and an attempted murder charge could send him away for years. Dad stayed on the run for about 2 months before turning himself in. He was tired of running and wanted to help get the charges on his dad dropped. He told Detective Randall that he shot Ricki on accident and felt sorry about it. He told him that his father wasn't there and had nothing to do with it. The charges against my grandpa were dropped. My dad pled to first-degree assault and was sentenced to 9 years.

"The psychological makeup of poverty has never been defined. Psychologists, economists, and sociologists have never coined the psychological mind state of a person or a family unit who suffer. According to Maslov's "Hierarchy of Needs", it is suspected that major pieces and connections to each of the needs are missing or not being met. But the resilience of an individual, whom is lacking in more than one area of need, finds those areas to be unimportant and expresses a higher level of value in the areas that are presently being fulfilled. From my experience as a child living in poverty in the 80's, safety, love, and esteem were the components that we cherished."

Life Without Dad

1983 - 1987

They sent my dad to the big house - Walla Walla State Penitentiary. My mom was a frequent visitor for the first year or so. My brother Tyree was born shortly after he got sent up. Mom would haul us up to the prison to visit my dad once a month. My parents ended up getting married and were able to have conjugal visits. There was a bus that would pick us up from downtown Seattle and take us to Walla Walla. We lived between my Grandma Lee and Grandma Johnnie's houses until my mom got her own apartment. Both places were cool to me. I liked staying at Grandma Johnnie's because she spoiled me. There was always food in the refrigerator at Grandma Johnnie's and she gave me a dollar every day. A dollar stretched pretty far in the 80's. Kind of like how five dollars stretches now. I liked staying at Grandma Maureen's too, because my grandpa had a lot of stuff for me to get into. Also, my cousin Jay, who was my Uncle Jerome's son, stayed there. He and I were only three months apart and we were tight like brothers.

My mom found us an apartment in the CD, right off of 26th and Lane. This was around 1984. It was a cool little two-bedroom apartment with a reasonably sized backyard. I met some kids in the neighborhood and we would ride our bikes all over. I had a cold speech problem that made certain pronunciations difficult for me. If I couldn't correctly pronounce some of my friend's names, I'd just make a new name for them. My favorite friend was a bald-headed boy named Marquis. But I called him "Skitched-Head Boy" because of the marks he had on his head. He was a couple of years older than me and lived across the street. He always had cookies, Twinkies, or cupcakes when he came outside. We were very inventive back then. Skitched-Head didn't have a bike to ride and always had to share or borrow someone else's. We found a bike frame and it motivated us to search the neighborhood for the rest of the parts to make him a bike. We even spray painted it so that people couldn't tell that it was made from spare parts. We got into a lot of trouble. Skitched-Head Boy was bad as hell. He liked to steal from the corner store and throw rocks at moving cars. I was too scared to do shit like that because I didn't want my mom to find out. Mom had a part-time job and even took a stab at a technical school. She had a lot of trouble trying to make ends meet. She found herself going to the food bank at the end of the month because she hated asking her mom or Grandma Maureen for help. Grandma Johnnie was a little upset at my mom for having two kids and getting married to a guy she knew was going to end up in prison. Grandma Maureen loved my mom and wanted us to stay with her. Grandma Johnnie always told my mom how hard it was going to be to raise two boys on her own. My mom knew it was going to be hard but she aimed to prove her wrong.

It was the Fourth of July and we went over to my mom's friend Laverne's house. Laverne and my mom went to high school together and were very close friends. They were close enough for us to call her Auntie. She had two daughters, Nikki and Pearl, who were the same age as Tyree and I. They lived right up the street so we went over there often. Us kids would be in the back room playing while the grownups would be in the living room smoking weed, drinking, and kicking it. Laverne's boyfriend, Michael, had a brother named Craig who was very fond of my mother. He was a lot shorter than my dad, and was nowhere near as well groomed; but he was cool. We would see him over there all the time. I remember waking up one morning at our house and seeing him in my mom's bed. I remember being kind of pissed off and confused about it because I had never seen my mom with any other man besides my dad. I didn't know much about sex, but I knew what went on when two adults were in the bed together. To the best of my memory, I don't remember ever seeing Craig leaving after that. The day that he came was the day he stayed.

In the early days of Craig being around, I remember not liking him. He wasn't mean or anything. He just wasn't my dad. As the days went by, Tyree started talking and calling him dad. I made him stop because he wasn't our dad. Even though he was the only father he really knew, I felt it was my job to let him know who our dad was; and it wasn't him. For the first couple of months of my mom and Craig's relationship, we still went to visit my father up at the penitentiary. Each time, before we got there, my mom would say, "Don't be running your mouth to your dad, Ty." I knew that meant, "Don't mention anything about the nigga she had in her bed while my dad was behind bars, thinking she was out here being faithful." I was only five years old but I knew it was wrong. My dad and I were pretty close. I was his oldest son and had his name. I already had a trait in me to keep it real with him. He always told me that I could always be upfront with him. He told me that he would never be mad at me or punish me for telling him the truth. I never lied to him or held anything back from him. He used to tell me that I was his best friend and I loved that.

In November of 1984, we were up at the prison for a conjugal visit. My dad and I were playing with some wooden airplanes that he helped me build. I just started kindergarten and Dad was asking me how I liked school. He noticed something was different about me because I was acting distant. I liked school and wanted to tell him all about it. I wanted to tell him how they were teaching me things that I already knew and how I was excelling in math. He needed to know all of this but there was something he needed to know even more. I was scared of how upset everybody was going to be if I told him about my mom and Craig. My mom was going to be mad at me, my dad was going to be mad at my mom, and we probably would end up not coming to visit him anymore. I also thought if my dad found out another way, and learned that I was holding out, he'd be mad at me, too. That would be the worst feeling of all. So, I told him and surprisingly, it didn't turn out that bad. Dad was hurt but he understood. He knew it would eventually come to this. Mom was a woman with two kids and needs of her own. Dad knew he was gonna be gone for a while and asking my mom to wait for him would've been asking for too much. Mom was young, beautiful, and not even in her prime yet. He figured that us kids needed a father figure in our lives, too. He knew that there were things we needed to learn that only a man could teach us. We shouldn't have to suffer because of him not being there. He promised to call and write us, but I didn't hear much from him for a while after that last visit.

    It was the mid-80's and we were living in the projects, Holly Park, which was located in the south end of Seattle. This was probably some of the best times of my life. Yeah, we were poor, didn't have too fresh of clothes, and we stayed getting into trouble. But shit, everyone else was going through the same thing. I had a bunch of friends all over the projects and we had something fun to do every day. There were a lot of Asians in the projects around this time. They were cool for most part. I had friends like George, who lived across the street. He was an only child. His mom was this crazy white lady and she used to always yell at him. He'd scream back at her ass sometimes and call her names because he was bad as fuck. His dad had passed away when he was younger. I think his dad was killed or died from drugs? He always talked about how cool of a guy he was. Phillip, who lived next door on our right, was another only child being raised by a single-mom. He was bad as hell too. He was always flashin' on his mom, cussing her out, throwing shit, and constantly running away. He would never stay gone for very long. What I remember most about his mom is that she talked really, really fast. It was *so* hard to keep up with her whenever she spoke. There was a Cambodian family that lived to the left of us and one of the kids name was Seak. Seak had a lot of brothers and sisters but he was as cool as they came. He was very athletic, able to do crazy gymnastics, and showed us some martial arts stuff that he knew. We called it Kung-Fu back then. There were a couple of other guys who strung along but the four of us were almost always together. My little brother, Tyree, would hang out with us sometimes, but not when we were planning on striking somewhere far, or were planning on getting into trouble.

We were into all types of shit just like real project kids. We built club houses, went on hikes in the bushes, broke windows at construction sites, stole shit from the grocery stores, played hide-and-seek, and harassed all of the girls who lived in the projects. I remember water fights, ranking contests, and free lunch programs at the local community centers. We'd get there as early as possible to get a free lunch so that we could hurry up and run to the other community centers down the way and grab another free lunch.

Craig and my mom were still together and she was pregnant with my brother Thomas. Craig and I got along for the most part but I hated it when he would tell me what to do. "He wasn't my dad and he couldn't tell me what to do", I constantly thought to myself. I would never tell him this aloud because he'd get angry, loud, and would give me this cold glare. I didn't like it. I mean…he didn't spank us or anything. The most that he would do is thump us on the forehead. That shit hurt! But Craig wasn't mean; he was just stern. I'm sure that there were times when we needed to be checked but I never considered us as bad kids. We got into a lot of shit, but so did the typical, average kid in the projects. However, I did talk back from time-to-time. I called it being "argumentative", but my mom would say, "You got a smart ass mouth! Don't get popped in it!" My mom did a lot of threatening but she never spanked us. Lord knows we needed it at times. Mom would always say, "My mom never whipped me, so I don't whip my kids." Back then, being a smart-mouthed kid wasn't as tolerable as it is today. Adults hated that type of behavior from a kid. To most adults, it was a form of disrespect. I got better at it as I got older.

My brother, Thomas, was born in 1986. I wouldn't know until a decade or two later that this was the peak of the crack-cocaine era. I saw my mom and Craig drink alcohol and smoke weed; but I never thought anything of it. Shit, most adults that I knew *at least* did that. I only heard about crack-cocaine from watching T.V.

We were considered poor around this time but we never had too many worries as kids. Mom and Craig were both unemployed and mom was on welfare. She got a check and some food stamps at the beginning of the month just like everyone else in Holly Park. On the first of the month, my mom would take us out with her to pay some bills, go grocery shopping, and usually to one of our favorite Chinese restaurants for lunch. Sometimes, we would go by Woolworth's or Sears and she would let us pick out a toy or something. Usually, things were the tightest during the last 10 days of the month. Food was scarce and we had to borrow money for food or go to one of the local food banks. I hated going to the food banks with my mom because I was afraid that one of my friends would see me there. I didn't want anyone ridiculing me for being seen at the food bank. Whenever things got really bad, my mother would get help from her mother, Grandma Johnnie. She didn't like to ask her mother for anything because she always had a long "How did we get here?" speech. She would always give us whatever we needed and never denied us anything. She even stopped by from time-to-time to make sure we had the essentials. If Grandma had known how bad things were at certain times, she would have been upset at my mom for not coming to her sooner. Grandma Johnnie was an angel. She would help *anyone* in need. She'd cuss you out first and then try to help you formulate a way to not get stuck in the same predicament in the future; but she would always help.

Things were going pretty well at school. I was in the second grade at Van Asselt Elementary. I was one of the smarter kids in class but I had a bit of a temper. I would get into fights with the other kids over the littlest things. I would always get mad whenever someone would talk about my mom. Kids were playing the dozens a lot back then but I wasn't into it, nor did I have the ammunition equipped to engage. I excelled academically. Van Asselt was kindergarten through third grade. I remember winning the school spelling bee when I was in the second grade. Winning made me feel smarter than everyone else; but not better. I took a lot of pride in my schoolwork because it was the *one thing* that I felt I could do better than most of my peers. Back in these days, I never knew about systematic biases or being disproportionately represented, but I knew that we had the odds stacked against us from the jump. I was in the third grade when I first learned about slavery. I was shocked and astonished, and I totally over-reacted. I ran home and told my mom about it. I said, "Did you know that we used to be slaves for white people?" She said yeah. I remember being genuinely upset that neither she nor anyone else in our family ever told me about slavery before. Here I am being all nice to white people when I should've been mad. I learned that slavery took place over 100 years ago and how things were much better now, but I was still passionately pissed. Things started to make sense to me. I saw situations where White people got certain privileges over others or were treated better, but it never dawned on me. I always thought that it was just because their skin was lighter. I witnessed a number of circumstances that led me to believe in the "lighter is righter" concept. The lighter-skinned girls were considered prettier, and the girls were more attracted to the lighter-skinned boys. This was during the El De Barge and Al B. Sure era. Finding out about slavery and how things went down back in those days helped me understand different life circumstances; and I was eager to learn more. My hostility towards this issue died down after a while. I realized that I wasn't able to make that big of a difference at that time. My education on the issue wasn't up to par and my soap box wasn't big enough. I was a project kid with the attention span of squirrel.

 I started playing organized sports and engaging in different types of martial arts disciplines. Seak had an uncle who taught us Tae Kwon Do once a week. Most of the kids only went every now and then, but I went frequently. I was kind of scrawny and smaller than most kids my age, so I figured that I might need to know this more than they did. Basketball was my sport and I loved being a part of a team. I played for the community center and we usually played against the other community centers around town. I knew everyone on the team because we all lived in the same projects or went to school together. My mom and Craig would sometimes show up to my games, but not regularly like some of the other parents. I used to think, "What could be so important for them to miss my game?" I never let it get to me because I had fun playing. I didn't know the role drugs played in their lives back then, or the significance of their lifestyle.

Van Asselt Elementary School was literally two blocks away from our house. Tyree and I used to walk to and from school together. When I started the fourth grade we were bussed to a school named West Woodland Elementary, in Ballard, which was in the northeastern part of Seattle. I never understood this at the time. There were plenty of schools within walking distance of our house, but they decided to waste time and resources to bus us way out north. I met a bunch of White kids and started to mingle with other races more. In Holly Park, and the surrounding neighborhoods, most of the families were Black. There were just a few White families, and a bunch of Asians. Even at Van Asselt, Blacks were the majority. At West Woodland, I was a minority and it felt weird. I had a good time there and met some pretty cool kids because I always came off as friendly. I didn't get into as many fights there because the atmosphere was different. No dozens being played, no one was trying to pick on me, and no one was trying to make fun of my clothes. Those White boys knew better!

Seattle started seeing the emergence of gangs in the mid-late 80's. I heard about the Crips and Bloods from some of my friends in the neighborhood, but I didn't know how serious this shit was until I watched the movie "Colors". This movie changed my view on what I thought about life. It had a powerful influence on me and my surroundings at the time. It was red for Bloods and blue for Crips. I had a couple of older friends who already chose to represent the Crips, and others that chose to rep with the Bloods. It momentarily became racial because most Bloods were usually Asians or Samoans. A few of them were Black, but only a few. My friends and I were too young and too scared to choose a gang back then. In the movie "Colors", they were killing each other over a color; and little kids were not excluded. In Seattle, people were getting shot for wearing the wrong color in the wrong part of town. A majority of the people who got shot weren't even in a gang. They were just at the wrong place at the wrong time or had on the wrong color that day. I knew a few people that started to represent a side, and even bought guns to protect themselves. During this time, a lot of people that I knew either got shot, killed, or went to jail because of gang-related crimes. I learned that there was nothing sadder than the funeral of a slain child, no matter the circumstances.

> *"We define what a family is and what it looks like. We are able to decide the necessary components of what we call family. No family is fully functional. The "dysfunctional" family can be used to describe any unit that is made up of many parts. Dysfunction means something that isn't operating correctly, but is still functioning. We let society describe how things are supposed to coexists. Anything that isn't performing correctly or according to what society deems as "normal" standards, is labeled as dysfunctional."*

Ball Til' You Fall

1988 - 1990

We had been going over to my Grandma Maureen's a lot. My cousins, Jay and his sister Jewel, were always there and we always had fun whenever I came over. Jay and Jewel eventually started living with Grandma and Grandpa because their mom was too far into her drug addiction and my Uncle Jerome was in prison for shooting someone. The state was going to place them into foster care but Grandma and Grandpa stepped in.

My Auntie Vernice met a man named David and they had a baby together. Around this time, Uncle Tommy was starting to get into trouble with the law. He was always getting involved in botched robberies or hopping into a car with one of his friends without knowing that the car was stolen. He hadn't been to prison yet because he knew how disappointed Grandpa would be if he ended up there. He actually wasn't a bad kid. He just always ended up hanging with the wrong people or was in the wrong place at the wrong time. I remember Uncle Tommy as being your classic "fat ass". He always seemed lazy to me. He was kind of a momma's boy, too. He was always at home, had a room full of shit, and was always eating something or playing video games. He was my guy though. Whenever we went to visit Grandma and Grandpa, he would take Jay and I to the backroom, hold us down, and let Tyree beat up on us. Tyree used to always complain to him about how we'd pick on him and not let him hang with us. He bonded with Tyree because he knew how it felt to be the little brother. Of course I would fuck Tyree up after we left, but he was happy that Uncle Tommy gave him the opportunity to get his in too.

Uncle Shelton was the only one who wasn't there. He joined the Army when he got out of high school and married his high school sweetheart. They had a baby together and moved to Oklahoma, where he was stationed.

My mom hadn't taken Tyree and I to see my dad ever since I told him about her and Craig. He hadn't called our house either. I talked to him once or twice when I was over at Grandma Maureen's house visiting, but it was never for that long. Every now and then he would send Tyree and I some mail that contained a short letter and some really nice drawings. Dad was one hell of an artist. Mom always said that he was gifted but he never focused on those attributes.

Uncle Jerome got out of jail but fell victim to drug addiction shortly after being released. He was a violent addict. He'd go in and out of jail for all sorts of shit. His addiction led him into doing some unspeakable things. My mom said that he was the type of person to walk into a convenience store and snatch up the entire cash register and walk out. He stood six feet tall and was about 300 pounds. He never combed his hair or changed his clothes whenever he was on a run and had a really creepy look to him after a couple of days. Other than that, he was actually a cool guy. He was goofy, easy to get along with, and had a great sense of humor. Once drugs entered his system he'd turn into a criminal. One time, he shot a man in the neck over a disagreement they had regarding how they were going to divide some loot after a robbery. The guy was actually a good friend of his. The guy survived and Uncle Jerome did time for assault with a deadly weapon.

Grandpa was slowing down because of his age but still acted edgy at times. He was still hanging out with his biker buddies but wouldn't stay gone quite as long. He was spending more time at home with Grandma, taking care of Jay and Jewel. Grandpa may have seemed crazy to most, and completely deranged, but he had a really soft spot in his heart for his grandchildren. He would give us anything. He taught Jay and I some stuff that our dads missed out on teaching us due to them being incarcerated. He took us fishing, let us help him repair some things on his old cars in his garage, and would even let us ride on the back of his motorcycle sometimes. I've heard plenty of stories about some of the crazy things he did, but us grandkids never witnessed that side of him.

It was spring of 1988. Tyree, Jay, Jewel, and I were in the living room of my grandma's house playing with Legos when this dude just walks in! We were pumped to see him! I knew that he was getting out soon but not this soon! When he got released from the joint, family from all over came to see him. Even the family that lived out of state made the trip to come and see him. He was the first one in the family to do such a long stretch. Plus, he was Tyrome! Everyone loved him! He was known as one of the most charismatic guys around town. It was a celebration! People barbequed, had cookouts, and were happy that a real one was home free!

I was about nine years old when my dad got out of prison. We sat back and had a long talk because he heard about how things were with my mom and Craig. Back then, I didn't care too much for Craig. I was tired of him telling me what to do and thumping me on my forehead, so I told my dad all about it. He said, "First of all Son, that's your step-dad. When he tells you to do something, you need to do it. Quit being so stubborn. I might have to talk to him about popping you upside your head, but your little ass probably needs it. I'm not gonna go over there and start nothing with him when he's been there for you while I've been locked up. That'll be disrespectful. I'm gonna thank him." Things like this made me realize that my father was cut from a different cloth. I wanted him to be mad and say that he was gonna go check Craig. But it made me feel grown to understand where he was coming from. Later in the conversation, I asked him, "Whachu gonna do now that you're out, Dad?" I was hoping that he would say that he wanted to live a normal life, get a job, or something else productive. Anything except doing something that would send him back to prison. My dad looked me directly in my eyes and said, "Son, I'm gonna get rich." I didn't know exactly what that meant. But I would soon find out.

 You have to understand what 1988 was like in Seattle. We were smack-dab in the middle of the crack-cocaine epidemic. It was a problem that would affect the Black community for years. The fact that it had reached the suburbs and White folks were being affected by it too, made it an epidemic. Before then, it was just a problem - a social issue in the Black community. Everybody was either doing it, selling it, or had some kind of association with someone involved in the dope game. My dad knew a lot of people, and from what it seemed, he did his proper research while behind bars. He got in the game and grabbed it by the neck! He applied pressure to the Seattle streets with little resistance. He claimed the game and had intentions of rectifying his hustle. His mission was to be the town's finest!

 "The human brain is comprised of many parts, such as, the cerebellum, cerebrum cortex, frontal lobe, etc. The brain also produces chemicals that

flow through various sections that make brain activity functional. These chemicals provide feelings, thoughts, make up the rewarding, fight or flight mechanisms, and influence human response. These flows are created during the critical thinking stages of the human mind and these chemicals are important in conducting brain wave activity. The chemicals that the brain produces are called dopamine. When you experience an exhilarating feeling of excitement or anything that produces an adrenaline rush, the feeling that makes your heart rate rise and gives you that "whoa!" feeling, is a chemical known as dopamine being rushed through your brain. This is a natural chemical that your brain produces on its own. When you snort or free-base cocaine, you experience the same feeling, only intensified. Crack-cocaine makes individuals experience an increased amount of a dopamine rush one never knew existed."

In the mid-80's, crack made its debut to the world. It was cocaine cut and cooked into a rock form that was smoked, instead of snorted or free-based. It was highly addictive and cheaper than the powder form of cocaine. It delivered a more intense amount of dopamine for a shorter amount of time. This is what made it so addictive; the fact that it was stronger, but the high didn't last as long. The most addictive attribute of crack is your first hit. The first hit that you take will be the best hit ever. This feeling of euphoria cannot be explained in layman's terms, but can probably be visualized by some kind of erotic animation involving climatic colors during an orgasmic experience. But you only get that feeling one time during your addiction; that is during the first hit. People spend their whole life trying to get back to that feeling but rarely come even close. Yes, heroin had an effect on the community and debilitated men, women, and families, but at some point, heroin use stabilized due to the progression of new laws, accessibility, and the development of opioid substitutes. Crack was cheap and easy to get because everyone had it. People's addiction intensified to the point where they gave up everything they had for a hit of crack-cocaine. I've seen people sell all of their possessions just to get it. Some women got to the point where they sold their bodies for crack. Some men even did some humiliating things that they would normally never do. The crack epidemic demoralized the very fabric of the Black community and nulled everything that our people fought for in the 60's and 70's. It was sickening.

It didn't matter how crack-cocaine was introduced to the communities, someone was going to profit from it. Although it affected the Black communities the most, we weren't the ones shipping cocaine here from South America, or processing it from cocaine to crack. Many people profited from the epidemic. Some people were turned into kingpins behind elaborate distribution schemes. As the problem grew, so did the demand. Neighborhoods became ran down, violence erupted, and crime went through the roof. Crews and gangs got into the trade and brought new insight on dominating distribution. It was communal deterioration in the form of capitalism, produced by entities formed to prevent epidemics like this from occurring. I was a child during the core development of this crisis. There hasn't been a governmentally induced genocide since Khmer Rouge's Cambodian genocide or Hitler's extermination of the Jews in WWII. The stronghold was only a breach in the opening of the floodgates.

We still lived in Holly Park in 1989. Dad had been out for about a year. I knew that he was doing his thing but we didn't see him much. When he did come by, he'd be draped in jewels, wearing designer clothes, and driving something really fancy-like. He would drop off money and clothes for my brother and I, sit back and chop it up with my mom and Craig for a minute, and then bounce. He would come by and pick us up from time to time but would eventually drop us off at Grandma Maureen's house or back at home later. He had a penthouse in downtown Seattle with one of his chicks that used to do runs for him. Her name was Jackie and he ended up marrying her after he got her pregnant. They had a daughter shortly, thereafter. We heard about Jackie and I remember my mom calling her a gold-digger. She didn't call her that out of hate or spite. She said this because she was known to only date men that had money. I mean…she was pretty and all, but that was all that she had going for her. I remember seeing my little sister a few times when she was a baby. She was a beautiful baby with a round face, just like Tyree. Her name was Ta'Kari.

Grandpa's behaviors may have settled down as he got older but he still caused a lot of ruckus after coming down from a run. He fought with Grandma often, which led to my dad getting involved. Dad bought a house out south for the sole purpose of getting his mom away from his dad, but it didn't last long. Although, Grandpa was pushing sixty and had some health issues of his own, he went searching for them with his shotgun in tow. Eventually, he found them and claimed his stake. Pops was knee-deep in the dope game at the time and had all the reasons necessary to not get involved in another war with his father. With all of the illegal business he was doing, the last thing that he needed was a crazy old man chasing him and his partners around with a shotgun. He gave in and compromised with him. He made peace with his father; not knowing that he wasn't going to be around much longer.

As my dad's hustle game flourished, so did the family's lifestyle. During this time, he established a crew. His crew was made up of some of his closest friends, longtime affiliates, and people that he met along the way of getting himself acquainted in the game. He trusted these cats for the most part. Everyone in the family was involved in the game with him to some extent. Grandma Maureen managed the money and kept everyone in check. Grandma had a brother, Uncle Mickey, who had a successful construction company. Grandma, Uncle Mickey, and my dad were able to launder a good portion of his drug money through it. Auntie Vernice was the chef. She developed a recipe to whip shit into shape in a quantitatively and qualitatively manner, while keeping the product profitable. Uncle Jerome tried to get his shit right but always ended up in some kind of conflict behind some senseless act. He was a brute. Whenever things didn't go right, he would always resort to physical force or violence. This led to him getting into fights and multiple shootouts. Dad gave him a smaller role in the distribution part of his operation so that if he fucked it up it wouldn't affect everything else he had going on. My mom and Craig even got involved a little bit, but their business together never mixed very well. My brother and I went from Payless shoes to the latest Jordans overnight. Our clothes game improved and we were even able to have a couple of bucks in our pockets from time-to-time. Uncle Tommy finally made it to prison. He was involved in a robbery with his friends and a few of them ratted him out to shorten their own sentences.

    My dad opened up a jewelry shop, a car dealership, and tried to partner up with a guy who ran a real estate company. The only reason why he didn't partner up with the guy was because he found out that the real estate guy was even more crooked than him. But he still did business with him in order to acquire some properties. He used them as stash houses rather than fixing them up for re-sale. Dad had a bunch of haters and people who didn't like him. My dad was as flamboyant as they came but was always willing to help someone out if they wanted in. This was an easy game and he felt that everyone should have a shot at it. He encouraged people to get in the game with hopes that they would end up copping from him on their way up. But after a while, he became a victim of his own success. A couple of people tried to rob him but only made off with some jewelry or short change. That's when he would send the goon squad after them! Dad wasn't actually into killing but he wouldn't hesitate to order a hit. He had a few trustworthy people who did the shit for sport. He actually did time with these cats and knew a few of them from his childhood. They were really sadistic and liked to torture muthafuckas. After they did a job, they would report back to my dad and tell him how they brutalized and violated a particular individual. My dad never liked these meetings. Listening to them made his stomach turn but he couldn't show that kind of weakness because these dudes fed off of shit like that. He thought of it as taking the bad with the good. He kept these guys fed though. They were kind of like his invisible bodyguards. He never thought that he would be the type of person who needed a bodyguard but he wanted people to know that there would be consequences and repercussions for attempts made on him or his loved ones.

My dad was shot at on more than one occasion. This was always due to him talking down to someone who he felt was hating on him, and by flaunting his wealth in people's faces in the midst of an argument. My dad could have a foul mouth and really talk down to a muthafucka! I mean…he used belittling words and talked to a person so harshly, that it would be reasonable for a person to want to shoot at him! This was just a part of his flamboyant personality. Some called him an arrogant asshole while others referred to him as the coolest person they had ever known. He must have thought that I was dumb or too young to understand what he did for a living because he kept telling me that he worked in a sandwich shop. I knew that it was bullshit but it's what he wanted me to believe at the time. I enjoyed the times that we spent together to the fullest! My dad was the flyest person in the town and I was his son. Shit, I felt popular just because of that alone! If you didn't know who Tyrome Lee was, or that I was his son, then you were a fucking dummy! When we were out, Tyree and I dressed up just like Dad. We would wear the fly gear, jewelry, and gazelle sunshades.

My grandpa had a stroke and died in the winter of 1989. It was a shock to everyone because it happened so suddenly. I think that it hit Uncle Jerome and Aunt Vernice the hardest. She was a daddy's girl and he was the oldest. They both had significant relationships with him and felt like their lives would be incomplete with him gone. Uncle Jerome told us about Grandpa when he came to our house to pick up Jay. It put Tyree and I in a state of disbelief and misunderstanding. We didn't know what a stroke was or how one could die from such a thing? All Jay heard was "Grandpa is gone" and it was enough to bring him to tears. He developed a close relationship with him since Grandma and Grandpa got custody of him and his sister. I was hurt because I never lost anyone close to me before. I just tried to picture visiting Grandma's house without him being there ever again.

Auntie Vernice was a train wreck at Grandpa's funeral. She was inconsolable; belligerent grief to the point of stereotypical. No one else could grieve because they were too busy trying to hold her up and calm her down. My dad did his best to make it a joyous occasion. He bought his father the nicest casket, him and his wife Jackie were dressed in white instead of the traditional black funeral attire, and he didn't have any sad funeral music playing. He played some of his dad's favorite music to help cheer people up and remember the good things about him. Poor guy. He had no idea what he was doing but he tried. He tried to hide the fact of how hurt he was by his dad's passing. He started to regret all of the fights and shootouts that he had with his father. He knew his dad's anger towards him was only because he didn't want him to fall victim to the system. He lost a good father and the only formidable opponent that he could learn from. He was glad that he took that charge for his father so he didn't have to spend any of his final years in prison. He knew that the best thing that he could do now was send him away in style; a luxurious funeral service to say goodbye to the man that loved him the most.

The following year, the Feds came and they came for everybody! They arrested my dad, Grandma, Auntie Vernice, and a bunch of the members of my dad's crew. The charge was conspiracy for everyone except my dad. He was facing R.I.C.O. charges. For all of you dummies who don't know what R.I.C.O. is, it stood for racketeering and influencing a corrupt organization. This crime was originally designed by the federal government to knock off mob bosses for crimes committed by their organization's henchmen. The Feds had historically experienced hard times convicting high-ranking mob figures due to the code of silence. The R.I.C.O. law made it possible to press and stick charges on them due to their criminal influence and other connections to organized crimes. My dad was no mob boss but they knew that he influenced many people around the town. They knew that if they pressed him and some of the other major players with charges, they could offer them deals to get them to testify against major distributors. Realistically, all they had were drug charges. That's it. Everything else was hearsay or came from word of mouth with no corroboration. My dad wanted his momma out. She and his sister were the only ones that he bailed out.

    All of my dad's money and accounts were frozen. He made some phone calls to get funds to hire lawyers for him and his co-defendants, bail money for his momma, and funds to tie up any loose ends. The U.S. attorney wanted to charge him with 25 years to life. I never understood how you could get a life sentence for a victimless crime? He wasn't being charged with murder, rape, or child molestation. So how could they give a nigga life? They mentioned how he contributed to an epidemic and caused havoc among the community. This was a community that White folks didn't even care about at the time. They stayed out of the CD and urban parts of the South End, years before crack-cocaine even hit the streets! He wasn't responsible for bringing the shit in and surely didn't create or start this epidemic! Every time there was a problem in the community, my dad did his part to create a solution. He put money into the community and helped feed poor families on many occasions. None of this was allowed in court.

The truth came out in a suppression hearing; they wanted those above him. They wanted to know who was supplying the person who supplied him. This is where my dad had an advantage; he had no idea who that was. He was able to show prosecutors how small of a problem he actually was. My dad's main method of copping his supply was through public storage. He rented a storage unit and his connect would make monthly drop-offs. He would get a phone call twice a month; a day before it got there and an hour after it was dropped off. He would never meet his connection face-to-face. When these people heard that my dad got locked up, the storage unit was shut down and phone numbers were either changed or disconnected. They had to lower his charges because they thought he was bigger than he really was and racketeering couldn't be applied. It was a glitch in the legal system that was constantly overlooked. The Feds would watch a nigga making money, making drops, buying big whips and jewelry, and consider him a major figure. These were the pawns in the game; involuntary smoke screens. They were facades that contributed to hiding the real players. The players who didn't buy fancy cars or jewelry. Instead, they stayed behind the scenes and laundered their funds through property acquisitions, land development, and corporate and stock investments.

My dad wanted his momma and his little sister to be straight. He knew that all of his other patnas and co-defendants were looking into deals for themselves. My dad knew that he was going to prison and was more than likely going to have to plead to a sentence that had double-digit numbers. He proposed a deal to the prosecutor that would hopefully free his mother and sister from all of the charges. They were the only ones who weren't caught red-handed. They had minimal surveillance on them and little corroboration from the other defendants. The Feds knew that they couldn't stick racketeering charges on him, but conspiracy seemed more reasonable. He agreed to accept a 15 year sentence if they dropped the charges against his mom and sister. He told the Feds he wasn't testifying against anyone or giving any other sources of information. He just agreed to the terms and began his prison sentence. Grandma Maureen and Auntie Vernice went free.

"All the smarts in the world can't prevent someone from engaging in counter-productive behavior. You can be the best at what you know and an absolute idiot at what you don't. It all breaks down to how our decision-making mechanism is programmed and how impressionable we are to our own ignorance."

A Change in Scenery

1990 - 1993

The years 1990 - 1993 were turbulent times for my brothers and I. Although, I wouldn't know the severity of my mom and Craig's addiction until later, we were experiencing the effects. Grandma Johnnie may have grown tired of living in the house that she raised my mom and Aunt Lisa in, and wanted to downsize. She didn't want to sell the house, so she decided to move into a condo/apartment, and rented her house to my mom. This was cool to an extent.

The good thing about it was that we were moving from the projects into a house. This meant that I would have my own room. The bad thing about it was that I was leaving all of my friends that I became tight with. We also had to change schools because we would now be living in the Seattle's Central District (CD) instead of the South End.

Seattle's CD is where Blacks were once confined by discriminatory housing practices. It was a tightly confined community that expanded two miles east to west and north to south. The CD's scene was a lot different from the South End's. First of all, it was smaller, but it was closer to downtown Seattle. They used to have little beefs and feuds between the CD and South End that us younger kids knew nothing about at the time. It was all about representing your side of town. As the gang and drug epidemic grew, it became more territorial and deadlier. The CD had about five or six main blocks and three major roads. Martin Luther King Way traveled from the CD all the way out south. Both sides of town had their own drug and gang problems emerging, however, things in the South End were more widespread because of the larger territory. The South End was big enough for blocks to beef with each other. There were Crips and Bloods on both sides of town, but in the early 90's, Seattle started seeing the presence of Black Gangster Disciples (GD). This was a gang that originated in Chicago but quickly spread in Seattle due to their presence in the jails and prisons. Prison fads always hit the streets quicker in cities along the west coast.

I started the sixth grade at Eckstein Middle School. It was located in the north end of Seattle and it was cool for the most part. There were more White kids than Black kids because they were still busing us inner-city kids to schools outside of the area in which we lived. My Aunt Lisa went there when she was in middle school and told me that it was a good school. I focused well on my studies during my sixth grade year. I got into a couple of fights because a few people thought that I was a sucka or just didn't know me. It really just boiled down to me defending my pride and not trying to be a punk. There were a bunch of girls that I liked but I could never make up my mind. I would "go out" with a girl for week or two and then get tired of them because I started liking her friend or some other girl.

    My clothes game improved because when I wasn't at school, I was "candy selling". Candy selling was this hustle that started in the hood way before my time. It was when an older person would take kids over to the White neighborhoods and run a scam of selling candy that we purchased from the drugstore. We had speeches, licenses, and permits that made us look legit. We would tell people that we were part of a group that raised money for food programs and a host of other activities for under-privileged, inner-city kids to keep them off of the streets and off of drugs. We had a legit scheme and one would have to do some extensive investigating to find out that it was a scam. There were a lot of other crews that did the same thing but in different parts of town. This was a good way for us kids to make money. We were always guaranteed to come home with $20 - $50 a day. It also put money in the guy's pocket that took us out. This was usually another hustler from the hood who everyone trusted or was comfortable with sending their kids out with. All he had to do was buy the candy, supervise us, and receive his portion of the profits. After a while, us kids got smart and made a copy of one of the licenses and then we started going out on our own. We took the scam to different heights and different areas. There would be days when we would go out all day and come home with over a hundred bucks a piece. We would get lazy or too comfortable and not go for a while, or blow it all in a day or two and be back to being broke. We didn't know anything about stacking. Another hazard that Tyree and I experienced was our money mysteriously coming up missing at home. There were plenty of times that we would go to bed with $40 - $50 and wake up to most of it being gone. Mom and Craig had company over all of the time but claimed that they never knew what happened to our money. We were so naïve.

    Seventh grade was a little more exciting and controversial for me. My popularity grew because I started going out with a White girl named Kelli who was crazy over me. She was known for getting around in her sixth grade year but she shaped up. She was better looking now and loved her some Tyrome Lee, Jr. I was also recognized for my academic achievements. I earned all A's on my report cards in the sixth grade and they put me in advanced courses when I entered the seventh grade. So, instead of being in classes with mostly Black kids, I was placed in honors classes with mostly White kids. Yeah, my friends started calling me a nerd and shit but it didn't faze me one bit. I met some interesting people in those classes and had some fun times with them. I believe this was when I started to become more diverse as an individual. I had always thought that Blacks and Whites were meant to be separate and that certain powers were trying to put us together for reasons unknown to me. I just knew that I had a different perspective on life when I left the hood and went to hang out at some of my White friend's houses. They all had two working parents, a nice home, and a lot of other shit that my brothers and I could only dream of having. Whenever I came home from their houses, I would sometimes get depressed because of us not having the shit that they had.

This was the point of time when I knew that my mom and Craig had a problem that was progressing. Our water kept getting shut off at the house. It would be off for a couple of days and then Mom would pull some strings or get some money from Grandma Johnnie to get it turned back on. Sometimes, Craig would go outside and "jimmy" the meter and turn it back on himself. The water company would find out about it and come back and turn it off again. Finally, the water company came and took the whole meter out of the ground and the water stayed off for months. We had no way to wash our clothes, take a shower, or use the bathroom. The smell that resonated throughout the house became so unbearable that I rarely came home. I didn't understand why my mom wouldn't just go to Grandma and ask her for the money to get the water turned back on? I guess she was embarrassed about how bad things had gotten? Grandma was no fool. She knew that my mom had somewhat of a drug problem but she didn't know to what extent. It wasn't my mom's pride that got in the way. It was her being in too deep with her addiction and not knowing how to address or confront the problem. Help was readily available but she and Craig didn't know how to access it.

You see…the problem with addiction is the blindness that it causes. It makes one blind to the obvious or the variation of how important things are. When addiction takes control, it becomes your main objective; it's your focus. It doesn't mean that you stop caring for your loved ones or their well-being. It just puts one's mind in a place of unconscious selfishness that makes them unaware of how important their essential needs are. We've seen movies where mothers would do all types of crazy shit like sell themselves, sell all of their kid's possessions, and some would even sell their babies for drugs. That degree of addiction is mixed with a psychological disease that puts them completely out of touch with reality. Those people were considered as "dope fiends" and were disconnected in every dimension. My mother was an addict. She had a problem that she could control at times but there were times when she could only focus on her addiction.

    Midway through my seventh grade year, I met a White kid named Willie P. He was a new student who I didn't think anything of at first. After talking to him a few times during class, I found out that he was actually pretty cool, but bad as hell. He introduced me to a whole new level of mischief. Middle school was a closed campus. We couldn't leave the school's grounds during school hours and there were no visitors allowed. We had security guards who roamed the campus and teachers took attendance during each class. If you were absent from a class and had no viable excuse, you'd be put in detention or suspended if it happened more than once. One day, Willie was telling me about how he came across some merchandise from breaking into houses. He invited me to come along with him during school hours but I refused. I asked him, "What would happen if we broke into someone's house and the people came home?" He said, "You dummy! We'll go during the day when everyone is at work." I said, "But we're in school at that time." He said "So? We can leave at lunch and be back by fifth period. We'll miss fourth period and get lunch detention at the most. Quit being a pussy, T!"

The next day, we met up at lunchtime. Willie said, "You ready?" I said, "Hell yeah!" We snuck off campus and roamed the neighborhood for about an hour and a half. We walked through alleys and backstreets as he showed me how to break into houses. He also showed me how to avoid the houses that readily had alarm signs on or around their house. I was rattled, but I couldn't let this White boy know that I was scared. But he did know that I was brand new at this.

We broke into three houses and busted some shit out of some lockers at a private school down the way. We came out with about $300 in cash, some jewelry, and a bunch of other knick-knacks. I found this knife that I thought was pretty cool and couldn't wait to show it off at school. We got back to school just as it was letting out, and the hallways were full of students that were leaving to go home for the day. I was showing the knife to a couple of friends of mine and was saying how I would cut someone if they even *thought* about trying me. Jokingly, I grabbed a random White kid, put the knife to his neck, and said, "Boy, I'll kill you!" He was scared as hell! I told him, "I'm just fucking with you", and I let him go as me and my friends laughed about it. When I got home, I couldn't wait to tell my homies about what I did! They automatically thought that I was lying until I pulled out my wad of cash. Of course they wanted to know when they could come along. I knew these cats weren't ready for this kind of action so I told them, "I'll see what's up."

When I got to school on the following Monday morning, the principal, Mr. Hookfin, found me in the cafeteria eating breakfast. He told me that he needed me to come to his office. I had been in trouble a few times and the vice principal was always on my case during my sixth grade year, but I had settled down a lot during my seventh grade year. Mr. Hookfin was a very tall black man who had been working at Eckstein for decades. He was there when my Aunt Lisa was a student there in the late 70's. I had no idea what the principal wanted with me? He told me to sit down in his office and to wait a minute and that he'd be right back. The only thing that I could think of was that he was going to ask me where I was during periods five and six on Friday. That was when Willie and I went on our little adventure. While I was waiting for Mr. Hoofkin to return to his office, I remembered Willie saying, "If they ask you where you were, just say you played hooky and roamed the hallways. The most they would do is give you detention." That was no biggie. I probably needed detention to get caught up on some homework that I missed out on while skipping. As I sat there waiting on Mr. Hookfin to come back in, my mind was boggled on how I was going to explain my absences to him. Another kid walked into to the office and looked around for something, glanced at me, then left. I didn't think anything of it at the time. Mr. Hookfin came back about two minutes later and had the vice principal and two security guards with him. The security guards grabbed my backpack and asked if they could search me. I refused at first but had no choice in the matter. The police were called and they did an extensive search of my locker and my gym locker. I started thinking that someone found out about Willie and I leaving and breaking into houses. I didn't know what they were looking for but they didn't find shit. Mr. Hookfin asked me, "Tyrome, where's the knife?" I played super dumb and said,

"What knife? I don't know what you're talking about."

Apparently, the kid who walked into the office momentarily and walked back out had identified me as the person who put a knife to his neck and threatened to kill him. I didn't know how serious this was and I felt that all I had to do was lie, deny, and say it wasn't me. The problem was that I had a very distinctive hairstyle my seventh grade year. My hair was cut into a slope like a few members of the rap/singing group Another Bad Creation. I also had a small blond streak dyed in the front, just to stand out a little. I stood out alright! It was the one identifying mark that the victim remembered and I was the only kid in the entire school with this hairstyle. Still, I said, "It wasn't me." I figured it was my word against his until I found out that they had a witness. After the witness identified me, I was immediately expelled from school and this incident was put on my permanent record.

When I got home my mom was furious! She was upset at the fact that I was expelled. But she was even more upset at the circumstances. I lied to my mom, so truthfully. I was expelled from what I had led her to believe was a false accusation. My mom felt like Mr. Hookfin put very little effort into investigating the matter and made a harsh decision that would follow me throughout the rest of my schooling. There were no conferences regarding the matter, no kind of formal investigation, I never got to face my accusers, there was no knife found, and most of all, they failed to contact my mother before making a decision. She immediately filed an appeal.

The following week, my mom and I met up with two school officials, Mr. Hookfin, and the vice principal for the appeal. They went over all of the details about the incident. I still stuck to my story: "It wasn't me." The school officials listened as Mr. Hookfin went into detail explaining what the victim and the witness said. He also went over all of the disciplinary infractions that I accrued since being at Eckstein. As one of the officials and the vice principal were going over some details, my mom asked, "Where are the accuser and this witness?" Mr. Hookfin said, "Mrs. Lee, they were both too scared to be in the same room as Tyrome." Mom felt that if you were brave enough to accuse someone of something so vile, that you should be brave enough to confront him or her in a controlled setting. I didn't know that this would play to our advantage. My mom, then asked, "So, Mr. Hookfin, I'm sure that you have not only their written statements, but also statements from them stating that they were too scared to be here because of Tyrome?" My mother counteracted them pointing out my disciplinary history by pointing out all of my accomplishments, my academic achievements, and the fact that Mr. Hookfin repeating what the victim and witness said, was hearsay.

Everyone left the room as the school officials pondered their decision. As we waited in the hallway, my mother spoke briefly with Mr. Hookfin and the vice principal. She asked Mr. Hookfin why he didn't look more into the situation before he made such a final, harsh punishment. She felt that as another Black man he should have put more effort into investigating the incident first, before making a decision to expel me from school. My mother asked him, "Why are you trying to make my son look like a troubled offender? Why didn't you mention the fact that he's been on the honor role since coming to this school and that he was put into advanced classes due to his academic achievements?" He had no legitimate answer for her and kept on explaining the seriousness of the matter and that there was a knife involved. She said very loudly, "What knife?! You never found a knife, you have a shaky witness, and your victim's story is bullshit! You should've done more!"

The school officials ruled in my favor. Their reason was that there was not enough evidence to keep such a harsh detail on my record and the statements could be considered as hearsay. The fact that the witness and the boy wouldn't tell their side of the story in person also played in my favor. They ordered that I be immediately enrolled back into school and that this incident be taken off of my permanent record. My mom and I left.

I felt liberated as we walked to the bus stop! I was pumped and felt like I had just beaten a murder rap. I chanted, "We won! We won!" as we walked down the street. Once we weren't in front of the school anymore, my mom slapped the shit out of me in the back of my head! I said, "What was that for, Ma?" She said, "Because you have nothing to be happy about! I know that you did that stupid shit, Tyrome! You lied and had me defend your ass like you were innocent! I know you did it! Don't fucking lie to me! Don't celebrate! Just be thankful that someone is always in your corner whether you're right or wrong!" I just looked at her as a tear rolled down my face. Not because I was hurt by the blow; but, because she was right. I lied all the way through. I lied so hard that I started to believe that I was telling the truth. I said, "Well, if you knew that I lied, why did you defend me and file the appeal?" She said, "Because you're my son. They had no evidence, a bullshit witness, and no real proof. When people accuse you of something they have to prove it and they didn't do that. A White boy said that a Black boy pulled a knife out on him and they ran with it without questioning any of the specifics." My mother never questioned my innocence. She asked me if I did it, I told her no, and then she went right into defense mode without ever questioning it again. One would have thought that she really believed that I was innocent of the allegations by the way that she defended me. It didn't matter. I was her son and she defended me no matter the case, and I loved her for it. I said, "You sounded like a lawyer up in there, Mom. You had Mr. Hookfin rattled." She said, "No, not a lawyer, Son. I just watch a lot of Matlock."

Eighth grade was a lot smoother. Someone called the health department because of the stench that was lingering around the house, due to not having water, the summer before school started. They notified the owner of the house, Grandma, and she couldn't believe it! She was hurt that my mom didn't come to her sooner. However, this was a problem that needed to be fixed. Grandma piled us up in her apartment for a month while she put things in order to have the house fixed up. She got the water turned back on, removed the old carpets, and had some cosmetic work done on the bathrooms. She also had some other minor changes done on the house that were long overdue. The biggest change that she made was her moving in with us. She knew that with her living in the house, things wouldn't get out of hand like before. This meant that my brothers and I would have to share a room again. I had mixed emotions about her moving in with us, but I was fine with it. Grandma was super cool. She wasn't too strict and would do just about anything for us. This meant that there would be more food in the fridge and people wouldn't be over as much. My mom and Craig still suffered from their addiction around this time, but they weren't as out in the open with it out of respect for Grandma's presence.

    I excelled during eighth grade. Everyone had gotten past the knife incident that happened the prior year, and I was kind of on the straight and narrow path. My grades were better, chicks were diggin your boy, my clothes game was up to par, and I had become one of the more popular kids. I always had money from candy selling but there was something new going on in the hood that could earn me some more money. It was 1993, and the Crips still occupied the part of the neighborhood where we lived. They pretty much had Cherry Street sewed up with the dope game. I knew a few of them and they were cool. We started shooting craps with the ones who were closer to our age. Once we started, we were hooked! We would always be on the corner, up in alleys, and behind buildings shooting dice. The police would always come after us but would only catch a few of us. If they ever had us cornered, we would just throw the dice and play dumb. On most days, I would break even from shooting dice but there were other days where I either got broke or came up. One day, I was up in the arcade shooting dice all day and night. I was there so late that Craig had to come and get me. This particular time, I was playing with the older Crips and I was on a roll. I had been there for hours taking all of their money. I was up about $1,000 when Craig came to get me. They didn't wanna let me leave until they got action at winning their money back. Craig said, "Fuck that! It's three o'clock in the morning and ya'll got my son up in here gambling! Ya'll should be ashamed of

55

yourselves! Let's go, Ty!" I was happy that he came to get me. I was on a mean streak of luck, hitting any and every point. I would have ended up taking even more of their money and making them even madder. Shit, I might not have made it out of there alive!

    Midway through my eighth grade year, my mom's younger cousin was released from prison. His name was Andre. He was my grandma's sister's son and he needed a cool place to stay in order for his parole to be approved. Andre was cool. I remember him being a prospect while in high school due to his athletic ability. He was a standout in football and baseball but he got caught up in the streets. He turned into one hell of a hustler and was well known around town. One of the stories that I heard about him was when he was pumping out of a crack house on Union Street. The spot was hot and got raided by the police one day but Andre wasn't there when they came. After they raided it, they boarded the house up and placed "Do No Enter" signs on the doors. Andre went there the next day, removed the boards from the house, put the door back up, and opened back up for business. People told him, "Yo, Dre! What you doing pumpin out of there again? The police were there yesterday. This spot is hot!" His response was, "Shit, of course it's hot! If it weren't, there wouldn't be any money being made here. Ain't nobody buying dope in Madison Park." Andre was a big dude and a good fighter. He went to prison for beating up two cops that tried to arrest him one day. He got sentenced to four years for assault on an officer. He nearly beat the case.

    Andre wasn't at the house much when he got out. He just used our house to stash his clothes and would come by early in the morning to shower or change. I was the only one awake whenever he came by because I was usually up getting ready for school. We talked during these mornings and he always talked about how smart I was. His closing remarks to our conversations were always something like "Stay outsmarting them" or "Don't let them outsmart you". I remember asking him why he always said that to me all the time. Andre said, "Because there's always gonna be someone bigger, quicker, stronger, or even more talented than you. You can't stop that. But you can make sure they're not smarter than you. You gotta use your head for more than a place to put your hat and stay outsmarting them." Those words would linger in my head forever.

One day, I came home from school and my mom, Craig, and Grandma were in the kitchen. My mom was crying. Craig was holding her and Grandma had a blank stare on her face. I asked, "What happened?" Grandma said, "Andre is dead." I asked how? And Grandma said that she didn't know. Andre was Grandma's first-born nephew. When he first started getting into trouble, he would stay with her from time to time. She practically raised him and he was more like a son to her. Apparently, Andre's car was found in Seward Park by an early morning jogger. The police were called because the jogger reported seeing blood leaking from the trunk. The police said that Andre was shot twice in the head and then stuffed into the trunk of his car. The killers were never found. The shit haunted me every morning because that's when I would usually see him. I hated walking around the house in the morning while everyone else was still asleep.

My grandma believed the police killed her nephew. She knew that they always had it in for him because he would always give them a hard time. Seward Park was a very popular hangout spot in the late 80's and 90's. After a couple of women were raped there, the police started closing the park at dusk and there was always police presence whenever someone tried to enter after hours. On numerous occasions, Grandma would drive there at night and try to enter the park herself. The police always stopped her. She would sit there, question, and scold the police after she was stopped. She would ask them, "Can you please tell me how my nephew could get a red and gold Benz in here at night but you continuously stop my blue Escort every time?" She did this a lot. Eventually, they put a restraining order against her that prevented her from entering Seward Park, altogether. She believed that they did this because they knew she was right. Grandma took the belief that the police killed her nephew to her grave.

Things were going a lot smoother towards the end of the school year. My brothers and I were doing cool, mom and Craig were still doing their thing (discreetly), and Grandma was living with us. She was usually there for just the middle portion of the day. She worked nights but she was always at church, Bible study, or some other church function. She loved playing bingo and hanging out with her church friends. She had an office on Broadway Avenue where she met up with clients a couple times a week. Yeah, she stayed busy. If there were any kind of traffic or activity going on at our house, it would be at night when we knew that she was at work.

I still played recreation basketball and football for the rec center but only for social reasons. All of my homeboys played a sport, I was good at it, and I had fun! My only issue was that I was always shorter than everyone else. There weren't a lot of people my age that were shorter than me. All of my homeboys had either gone through or were going through a growth spurt. I knew that I had some height eventually coming my way because my dad was six foot and so were my uncles. I was waiting, patiently.

"Does anyone know why one starts a sentence with a preposition? You give me an answer to that and I'll give you a legitimate explanation for how one may profit from his own despair. The answers are similar and coincide with one another. It's a rule, but not forbidden according to modern language. It may lead one to think that his actions differentiate from the ones of others or those that came before him. But in all actuality, our programming is set in neutral regarding ethical standards and we are always able to identify the prerequisites to our own downfall, while in motion, elevating towards the top."

Dad's Furlough

Summer of '93

I was at home speaking with my grandma in her room when he pulled up. He was in my Uncle Mikey's car. It was my dad and he was out of prison! We were pumped, confused, and surprised! He was just sentenced to 15 years, three years ago. I thought, "Did he break out or did they decide that all of that time wasn't needed? Was he such a model prisoner that they decided to release him early for his good behavior?" Sure, all three options were bullshit but I was just happy that he was out! We greeted him with joy and he seemed equally as happy to see us! We hopped into the car and rolled around with him for a minute. We talked about how things were going in our lives. I thought to myself, "To hell with all of that!" I asked, "How did you get out of prison so early?" He said, "I'm out on a furlough." I had no idea what that was. I asked if he had to go back and he said, "Eventually, but let's just enjoy the time that we have together right now." It didn't make sense to me so I just rode with it.

We drove around for a little bit before he dropped us back off at the house. I let him know about my eighth grade graduation and asked him if he was going to be able to come? He said, "Probably not, Son. But I can make sure that you are the flyest dressed mothafucka in the building!" He slid me and my brother a couple bucks a piece and told us he'd see us in a couple of days. He said that he had some business to take care of and if everything worked out, he could probably stay out of jail a little longer than expected.

It was spring of 1993 and I was at the end of my eighth grade year. We had an upcoming commencement ceremony for the eighth grade students who were graduating and heading to high school. I had a patna named June-Bug. We grew tight during our eighth grade year when he moved from Union Street over to Cherry Street earlier that year. We became gambling buddies. We made money betting on each other while shooting dice and would spot each other a couple of bucks when one of us was down. June loved fucking with the broads. I mean…I did too. But I liked getting money, playing sports, and getting my schoolwork done first. June always liked to go over to girl's houses and wouldn't go unless they had a friend for me. He was good at finding all of the easy girls and getting the so-called "good girls" to put out. If they weren't putting out, we weren't coming over or staying for very long. I got a lot of action fucking with June. We bought suits for graduation that were killing everyone else's. My suit was blue and his was white. We also had these hats made. Mine said "TLEE" and his said "JUNE".

After graduation, my mom and Sue, June's mom, threw us a little graduation party. It was cool because a lot of my friends from school came over. My cousin Nicki, my patna James, Tony, and a couple of other heads came through. My mom bought us bottles of champagne and she let us drink a little. We definitely overdid it! Half of us passed out by midnight and the others were too drunk to recollect. I knew that it was only champagne but it was the first time that most of us drank. This was a great way to celebrate graduating from middle school and entering into high school. Bon Voyage Eckstein!

My dad did stay out longer. He was actually around for most of the summer and I was with him a majority of the time. He took me with him when he went to meet some of his peoples. He tried to discreetly explain to me the business they did and fucked around and revealed to me that drugs were involved. I was no dummy and he knew it. I saw him making moves, meeting with people who I knew were in the game, and having hella money. There were times when he would have me hold wads of cash and he'd forget that I even had it. I would walk around with him for days and have two or three thousand dollars in my pocket that he totally forgot about. Whenever I reminded him of it, he'd say, "I know. Just hold onto that, Son." We were rolling around one time and I was listening to him talking on the phone, plotting on "changing the game". You see...I knew a little about the dope game. I knew that back then, they had $20 rocks. That's how crack was sold. Maybe every now and then you could get two for $30 but $20's were the basic monetary value of each stone. Then, I heard about "double up". That was when you could get double what you paid for. It didn't work for 20's though. You would have to buy $50 - $100 worth. So, if you spent a hundred dollars, instead of five 20's, you'd get 10. This was mostly for the people who were hustling or those trying to make a few bucks while still having enough to get high. You had to be pumping major work in order to sell double up and still make a profit. My dad started "triple up" and it only worked with people who spent at least a $100. This was the small time hustler's dream in the early 90's. They could actually see their money grow with this deal. People had doubts about it at first. They figured that the dope probably wasn't any good and that was why he was selling it for so low or that the stone stones were going to be really small. They were all wrong. Auntie Vernice's recipe was on point! The product was A-1 and the stones were fatter than the usual. When people asked my dad how he could pull off such a good deal and still make a profit, he would tell them, "Man, stay out of my pocket and respect the hustle." Most of the time, people wouldn't question him at all. They just loved the fact that a real nigga was out and he was flooding the town with good dope again!

    Seattle was jumping around this time. The streets were flooded with drugs and gang presence. It looked even crazier in the CD because it had become so concentrated. We lived off of Cherry Street where the Crips dwelled. They also occupied parts of Jackson Street, which was about six to seven blocks south of Cherry Street. Jefferson Street was one block south of Cherry. The Bloods had that blocked sewed up. There wasn't too much friction between the Crips and Bloods, contrary to what one would expect. They didn't mingle or anything. They just stayed out of each other's way. The real friction was between the Crips on Cherry St. and Gangster Disciples (GD) who occupied Union Street. Union was about 4 blocks north of Cherry. The origin of their beef was unknown to me. I think it may have been a territorial thing? Most of the Crips OG's were from California, and although the GD's gang originated in Chicago, the members in Seattle were homebred. So, it could've stemmed from a Cali versus Seattle thing?

"Dad, I want in." I was dead serious when I spoke those words. I thought about it long and hard and made sure that I was speaking with assurance. He said, "What little nigga?!" I said, "I want in. I don't wanna just hold your money. I wanna hold *my* money." He thought about it seriously and asked, "What do you know about this game, Ty?" I said, "Enough. I've been watching you for over a month now. If there's anything else I need or wanna know I'm sure you'll fill me in. Just put me on." After a few more days of me bugging, he put me on. He showed me how to whip it, cut it, bag it efficiently, and how to distinguish my profit from re-up. He broke the severity of the game down to its finest fabric. He said:

"This shit may look easy, son, but it's a dirty game. There's a lot more to this than just making money. There's rules and principles you have to live by and there's consequences if your game isn't up to par. You're gonna come across some crazy shit trying to get paid and you're gonna see some shit you'd thought you'd never see. People are gonna disappoint you and show you their true colors. You'll see the world for what it truly is. You're gonna change from a boy to a man overnight and you're gonna have to grow the fuck up. If this is for you, you

might last. If not, you'll humbly leave it alone or run the risk of turning into one of these crackheads. You better figure it out because I'm not gonna be here too much longer."

I listened to everything that my dad told me but my mind was bent on counting money and establishing myself as a hustler. I knew that most of what my dad was saying was the absolute truth. He knew he was gonna be leaving soon and I would be left out in these streets with some other dude trying to tell me the same thing. The only difference is that they would be schooling me for their own benefit. He kept reminding me to be my own boss and find a turf where I would be safe and comfortable. He never said anything about not being too flashy but I picked that up on my own. I did a little observation of him before I actually got into the game.

I remember when we went to pick up my dad's younger patna, Moses. He was one of his ex-girlfriend's younger brothers. He was a hustler who had a knack for grinding on any strip and making it his home until the work was gone. If the strip was still jumping, he'd re-up and do it all over again. But just as good of a hustler that he was, he was even more relentless as a shooter. Moses was rather small in size and wasn't that good of a fighter and he knew that. But he was known as a "banger" and wouldn't hesitate to let his pistol sing. He was 18 years old and had already done a stretch in juvenile detention. Everyone who knew Moses knew that he wasn't anybody to play with. The police considered him a suspect in a murder a few years ago but they didn't have enough evidence or a witness to make the charge stick. Moses was cool though. He was about five years older than me and I liked kicking it with him because he had a strong work ethic. He was the first person to give me firsthand knowledge on how to hustle in the streets. He took me to Union Street to get down. Union was the block where my dad, Uncle Tommy, and my cousin Andre made their bones. This is when and where I found out that EVERYBODY was smoking crack! A majority of the people that I encountered were associated with it in some way, fashion, or form.

My dad had a stash house on Aloha Street, which was about a mile north of Union. That's where Moses and I kept our drugs and where we would go to re-up. I remember we were chilling at the stash spot and we called a taxi to take us to Union. The taxi driver was an East African dude who spoke little English. I thought nothing of it. It tripped me out later on that day when he chased me down on Union to cop some work from me. That's when I knew that this shit was multi-dimensional. I thought only older people smoked it and the younger people just sold it. I found out that not all of the older people smoked it and there were some people my age that smoked it, as well. It was a harsh reality, but to realize that this shit was open to anyone thickened my skin.

About a month into my hustling, I felt good about myself. I had money and was able to buy myself some fly gear. I was having fun too! The dope was basically free because my dad had so much of it. Moses and I were making a killing on Union! I put a couple of my friends on just to prove that I had the ability to do so. Word got back in my neighborhood that I was doing big things. I was 13 years old, had a pocket full of money, and was rocking the latest gear. I hadn't been home in over a month because I was either on the block grinding or out with my dad. I mean…I went by to change my clothes every now and then, and we stopped by to pick up/drop off

Tyree, but I hadn't stayed there in a while. Mom and Craig were still doing their thing but they knew what I was up to. I wasn't fooling anyone. I tried my best to stay out of my grandma's way. She would've picked up on me immediately. I wouldn't have been able to lie to her or insult her intelligence like I did everyone else.

Dad said, "If you're gonna work with people in this game, you need to know what they bring to the table." He told me that Moses brought security. Dad knew that I would need that if he wasn't gonna be around. Moses knew a lot of people but not too many people knew of his dirty work. He had love for some of his real patnas and showed that love by putting in work for them. He showed me this one time. I was even forced to take part in it. Moses and I were walking back to Union from Cherry Street when we ran into one of his homeboys named T-Kid. I knew of T-kid through his younger brother whom I went to school with. T-kid was a real dude, but his younger brother, Trevor, was a punk who only got notoriety or respect because of who his older brother was. However, I'll get to that pussy later. T-Kid was limping down the block. He had a cast on his right arm from a car wreck that he was in, a week prior. But now, his face was banged up and he looked like he had been scuffed up. Moses went up to him and asked, "What happened, homie?" T-kid said, "Man, them Crip niggas jumped me in the park. Then they held me down and let the bitches stomp me out." Moses was furious. You see…we were G's. We followed the Black Gangster Disciple's code of conduct and principles and were loyal to one another due to the readings we were taught by the older G's. The Crips ran Cherry Street. A lot of them were from California and started their own faction here in

Seattle. The G's couldn't stand the Crips around this time. They tolerated the Bloods because they did business together but they rarely mingled with them. When T-Kid told Moses that some Crips jumped him, retaliation was imminent. We walked back to the stash house because that's where Moses' guns were. He grabbed one of his pistols; we hopped into his car, and headed towards the park where T-Kid said that he was jumped.

When we pulled up to the park, the Crips were still there. It looked like they were barbequing or having some sort of party. Moses asked T-Kid, "Are them the niggas right there?" He said yeah and pointed out the main culprits. Moses said, "I'll be right back. Ty, hop into the driver's seat." Moses hopped out and walked into the park by himself. When he got near the center of the park, he asked them, "Why ya'll beat down my homeboy? You see he had a broken arm and shit. What kind of hoe shit is that?" They didn't know Moses was a nut, nor did they take that probability into consideration. They just thought he was bold and stupid. One of them said, "Because he was being disrespectful to one of the ladies and talking shit." Another one said, "Because we felt like it. Why, whachu gonna do?" Those words assured Moses of his next move. He reached into his pants and pulled out a .45! They ran as he began blastin! I knew he hit a few of them because I saw them drop. After he emptied the clip, he started running back to the car. After he hopped in, I started the car up and drove off! He said, "Ty, mash this shit straight to the lake!" He wiped his gun down thoroughly and then broke it down into several pieces.

Once we got to the lake, Moses tossed the gun parts into different parts of the lake. We rode back towards the hood, parked the car, and took a cab back to the stash house. Moses made me promise not to tell my dad about what happened. He knew that my dad would be upset with him for having me involved in that kind of mayhem. I promised him that I wouldn't tell him. I actually got a rush from all of that action! I was the get-a-way driver and felt like a real gangster! I was pumped to have played a role in that shit!

I hadn't purchased a gun yet because I didn't feel like I needed one at the time. I felt the city knew who I was and knew there would be repercussions behind fuckin with me. My dad always had one with him because he had haters. He wasn't a fighter but people knew he was a shooter when he needed to be. Nobody forgot about the Ricki C. incident. Moses and I got into a little squabble and I called my dad to pick me up. We were out riding around and Dad started schooling me. He told me that I needed to keep the peace with Moses because that guy didn't have it all mentally. He always took the time to let me know more about the game. He felt that there was always more to know.

We were on Madison Street, about two blocks north of Union, riding around when a smoker flagged us down. He was a heavy-set Samoan man. He said that he wanted $50 worth. I had about that much on me because Dad just picked me up from the blade. I got out and tried to serve him but he snatched the work out of my hand and started walking off. I jumped on his back and tried to take him down but he threw me like a rag doll! He was twice my size and twice as strong! I couldn't find anything to hit him with so I tried jumping on him again and got the same results. The second time I tried, he threw me against a car and I banged my head. I was knocked out for about 10-15 seconds. Dad hopped out and started fighting with the guy. He was doing alright until the guy got a hold of him. I thought it was a temporary hold on him until I realized that my Dad couldn't get loose. I hit him over the head a few times but he wouldn't let my dad go! I thought he was gonna kill him! I ran to the car and grabbed my dad's gun. It was a little .38 snub nose. I pointed it towards the guy's back and without hesitation I fired two shots. My dad freaked! My dad snatched the gun out of my hand and yelled, "Get in the car!" He dropped me off at the stash house while he went to dispose of the gun.

When my dad returned he was furious with me. He said, "What the fuck is your problem? Why did you shoot him?" I said, "Because he was gonna kill you!" He tried to convince me that I took it way too far and his life wasn't in danger, but he could see that I wasn't convinced. I thought that he would've been proud of me. I truly believed that I saved my dad's life in that moment. He stopped panicking and talking, took a deep breath, and looked into my eyes as I sat there listening to him. He knew that I did what I felt I had to do. He felt telling me that I was wrong wasn't going to do me any good. He said, "Son, you've done something you can never take back. You're gonna have to live with this for the rest of your life. If the cops ever question either one of us about this, just deny being there and say that you don't know anything."

The next month the Feds did a multi-site raid on my dad's operation. The FBI, DEA and ATF raided the stash house on Aloha Street, an apartment that he had with one of his chicks, and Grandma Maureen's house. I had just left the stash house hours before the raid. When I left, Moses and one of his patnas were there asleep. When the Feds came in Moses started blastin'! I figured that he must have thought that they were robbers or something? Come to find out, he knew that it was the cops all along. He just happened to have his gun near him so he started shooting. Him and his patna were both wounded along with two of the cops. When they came to get my dad at my Grandma's house, they dug up the entire backyard. They heard rumors of my dad having money buried back there. They didn't find anything. They arrested everyone that was at the house: my dad, Grandma, Auntie Vernice, Uncle Jerome, and some of my dad's friends who were there. Shortly after the raids, I found out the reason why my dad was really let out of prison early and what a "furlough" was. I also found out that they had an informant named John. He was a customer who infiltrated my dad's organization by becoming a smoker and eventually, one of his workers. I actually spent some time with John running errands and shit. I never thought anything of him and he seemed cool. He turned into a runner and would run errands and drive us places if needed. He knew way too much and it didn't look good for my dad.

The truth behind my dad's release was due to a deal that he made with the Feds. While he was away, a few other players had moved up in the game and became hard for the Feds to touch or bring charges against. They tried, in multiple ways, to infiltrate their organizations but failed each time. They were smarter, more discreet, didn't leave paper trails, and were even more ruthless. These were people that my dad knew well and did business with before he went down in 1990. The deal that the Feds proposed to my dad was to put him back in the game as a major player. They provided him with $100,000 and 5 kilograms of cocaine to put him back in the game. They wanted him to do business deals with them and orchestrate controlled buys. They also wanted him to sell them the drugs that they were providing him. In return, the Feds were going to cut his sentence in half and give him back some good time he lost due to conflicts that he was involved in while in prison. My dad agreed to the deal but he welched. He met with the people that he was supposed to set up and told them what the Feds knew about them. He even told them about the deal he agreed to with the Feds. He advised them to take their earnings and leave town. They believed him because he was telling the truth and had no reason to make up a story like that. A majority of the guys packed up and left. My dad then decided to distribute the drugs that were provided by the Feds at the cheapest price possible, without much competition on the streets. He used the $100,000 for undisclosed purposes. He tricked out a few cars, bought some houses in Nebraska, and laundered some money through his Uncle Mickey's business. He had monthly meetings with the Feds and continually strung them along. He kept claiming that he was close to giving them what they wanted but he just needed more time. He bullshitted around with them and they bought it for about 4 months. When they finally caught on to what he was doing, they came for him full force. They brought him up on new conspiracy and racketeering charges. This time, the Feds weren't offering him any deals. He used what money he had to protect his mother from any charges, but he and everyone else had to fend for themselves this time. In the end, he received an additional 6 years to his sentence. I was left in the streets by myself.

"The phrase, "I'm a product of my environment", is a suitable explanation to why we do what we do, or why we are only capable of resorting to a specific style of socialization that we are accustomed to. You can take a monkey out of the jungle and place it into human civilization, but he'll still throw shit, find trees to swing from, and use the same form of communication taught to him in his previous environment. Genetics is a totally different story."

The Apple Doesn't Fall Far From the Tree

1993 - 1997

I started high school shortly after the raids. My dad was gone and so were most of his patnas. I felt lost for a minute but then I realized something: I had something that most kids my age didn't have…knowledge of the game. I had been schooled by one of the slickest players to have ever touched Seattle's turf. Around this time, there was a war going on between the G's from Union and the Crips on Cherry. I stayed away from all of the mayhem the best that I could. By then, the G's heavily influenced me, but I lived closer to Cherry where the Crips dwelled. I was cool with most of the Crips but my loyalty was with the G's. Eventually, the G's hit them hard by knocking off a couple of the older Crips and it kind of dismantled their unit of operation. Over the next couple of years, they dispersed from the Central District scene completely. I managed to stay away from trouble by playing football for the high school team during my freshman year and digging into my studies. I still slung dope but not at the magnitude that I was while my dad was out.

My mom and Craig knew what I did but they didn't trip as long as I kept my grades up. As time passed, I progressed deeper into the game. I became addicted to the street life. Money was coming fast and easy. I started spending more time on the block and less time in school. I mean...I still attended school but my grades were failing. I would often find myself trying to pull them up before the quarter ended. I knew a couple of people who could fill me in on what I needed, and had a friend in the attendance office who could alter my attendance record, but that didn't work for long. I bought a car halfway through my freshman year. I was one of the only 14 year olds in the town with a car. I was pulled over by the cops a lot because either they knew who I was or because I looked too young to be driving. After getting pulled over a few times for driving without a license, I decided to stop pulling over, altogether. This led to a few high-speed chases that I actually got away with a couple of times. When the cops did catch me, they would kick my ass and lock me up for a couple of days or until my mom came and got me from the precinct. I visited the juvenile facility numerous times but never for drugs. I went to jail mainly for driving, fighting, or eluding. When I was pumpin on the block I was focused. I would never stand on the block like everyone else, nor would ever have the dope on me unless I was making a sell. I had east coast tactics that people in my neighborhood weren't accustomed to. I saw a lot my homies catch dope cases by getting hemmed up for loitering and the cops would find the dope in their pocket or something. Fuckin dummies! I keep it too real! I didn't smoke weed on the block because I could always go home and smoke weed with my mom and Craig. My mom always told me, "Why smoke weed outside on the strip and risk going to jail or your weed getting laced? Smoke that shit at home where you'll be safe, with me." My mother and I got closer over the years and Craig was a huge influence on making me a more responsible hustler.

I usually copped my work from some of the older G's. I was still small-time but I was moving up. I copped quarters and half ounces hard because I couldn't find it soft. I remembered how to cook up because I used to watch my Auntie Vernice cook up some of my dad's shit. Cherry Street was jumping but it was mainly between 18th to about 28th. I lived on 31st, which was the more residential part of the neighborhood, because we had more White people up there. It still popped off but it wasn't as active as it was down the way. I was one of the few people hustling up that way. It didn't move as fast. But it moved.

Mom and Craig's friends started copping from me but I would never sell anything to my mom or Craig, directly. They knew that I wouldn't sell them anything. They found ways to get it from me anyway, by having their friends buy from me. I knew it was for them but I figured they were gonna get it from somewhere regardless of if I sold it to them or not. Back then I didn't know that by me slanging it to their friends, it was just the same as me slanging it directly to them.

I loved my mom. And even though him and I squabbled a lot when I was younger, I loved Craig too. He was there for me when my father wasn't. He kept it as real as possible. He taught me how to address my clientele and what to not go for. I remember he once said, "Set your own price for your product, boy. They gonna buy it from you one way or the other. Maybe not at first, but the shit don't spoil, rot, or mildew. The shit will sell eventually." Craig taught me how to be discreet and to not be involved with too many people. I mean…I had friends but I kept my business to myself; especially, while I was on the blade. I was lucky to have received game from a number of players in all areas of the game. As a matter of fact, I wouldn't even call it luck. Everyone had the same opportunity but just didn't have the patience or ability to listen. I took that shit in. I was always willing to listen and get my "boots laced" by the older folks. I remember my grandpa used to say, "Ears that don't listen to advice accompany the head when it is cut off." I never knew what that shit meant until I read it in a book while in middle school. It was an African Proverb. It helped me differentiate advice from criticism and to figure out when they were the same thing.

    I never knew what the qualifying factors were to being classified as an addict. At the age of fifteen, I knew there were only two types of addicts: crack heads and alcoholics. I also knew that just because someone was an addict, it didn't mean that they weren't capable of doing extraordinary things. It just meant they had an unaddressed issue. I've seen crack fiends get loose on the basketball court, pull off elaborate scams on intelligent people, or display superb fighting skills against well-known knockout artist. Some of the most intelligent, inspiring words I've ever heard came from the drunks that hung out in front of the corner store. Realizing this helped me heighten the respect that I already had for my elders. It would be years down the line before I learned more about being adequate despite one's imperfections.

My uncle Tommy got out of prison before my sophomore year of high school. He had been in and out of prison twice and missed out on a lot. My uncle wasn't a criminal per se. He was just a victim of unfortunate circumstances. While in prison, Uncle Tommy immersed himself really deep with the Gangster Disciples. He was a ranking member in prison and internalized all of the literature and philosophies of the gang. He had the oath and historical background memorized. A lot of people in the CD started claiming GD but it was only because it was the thing to be around those times. I mean…I admit it…I claimed like everyone else did. However, I wasn't banging as hard as the others were. I was more into reppin my hood, my block, and my district. When my uncle told my brother Tyree and I about what the Gangster Disciples were doing and what they stood for, we were eager to know more. One of the things that stood out most was that the GD's enemies were the Vice Lords and we didn't know a single one in town. After kicking it with him for a couple of days, Tyree and I decided that we wanted to be down with the shit. We wanted to solidify ourselves as GD's and not just be one of these other cats that were claiming it just because everyone else was claiming it. Uncle Tommy told us that he could bless us in and have us take an oath. The oath ordered us to stay true and sincere to the core values and principles of the Disciple's Nation. Uncle Tommy broke down the laws and the literature that had been bestowed by the GD's originator, Larry Hoover. That day, we officially became Gangster Disciples. It meant that we were part of something bigger than the Central District and bigger than Seattle. We were now a part of the Folks Nation.

High school was becoming more of a social event and an opportunity to sell some weed during school hours. I was attending just a few classes so I could keep the truancy officers off my ass. I was at my third high school by my junior year. I was kicked out of my first high school during my sophomore year because they claimed that I was contributing to their "marijuana problem". I earned the name "Ty-Budd" during my freshman year because I was Ty and always had bud. I was never caught selling, smoking, or possessing weed but everyone just knew that I was running the weed game at the school. I flashed on them one day in the office and they ended up calling the police on me. I was pissed at being accused of something without any valid proof. The principal, Mr. Howard, was from the hood and tried to have my back but his hands were tied when I started flipping and throwing chairs in the vice principal's office. I didn't like her because I knew she had it in for me. She was always calling me into her office for bullshit or for something she heard from someone else. Yeah, I was cursing mothafuckas out and just showing my ass. I wasn't arrested but the police escorted me off of the school's property and I was expelled.

I was really fucked when I had to go to an alternative school in the South End for the remainder of the year. I didn't have a lot of enemies in the South End but they knew I was from the CD. I tried to stay out of gang beefs because I was more focused on making money. I was just trying to hustle wherever I could and these chumps made it difficult with all of the turf wars. Plus, I had a lot of friends in the south that I went to elementary school with. I mean…there were a few "sandbox" homies that I was still tight with. Those bonds didn't break just because I moved to the other side of town. Shit, our parents still hung out together. But beefs happen and there were a few cats out there that just didn't like me. I called them "territorial" suckas who hated me for no real reason. Sure, I did my fair share of dirt to cats, but no more than what they pulled on me and my homies. I came to school with a pistol every day. They knew that I wouldn't have come there without one. I was only there for about three months and managed to not get into any really bad altercations. I kicked it with this cat named Jamal who I used to play little league basketball with when I stayed in Holly Park. Even though we were much younger back then, we were still cool. He became a high school basketball phenomenon and there were a bunch of colleges looking at him, but he had fallen behind on his grades. We had a few classes together and we used to always talk about our younger days. He wasn't a banger but he was cool with most of the people that I had problems with in the south. We made a deal: He wouldn't let them niggas try any funny shit with me while I was there and I would help him out with some of his school work. It wasn't that I needed his protection, but I'd rather use his influence than be forced to kill some niggas. Jamal ended up going to college for a year at Michigan and then got drafted to the NBA.

    I decided to go to Franklin High School for my junior year. Now I admit, I went there solely for the bitches. I knew Franklin had a bunch of fine ass, saddity broads that I could knock off while I was at school. Plus, I heard they didn't have a real weed man and I planned to fill the position. But Franklin was a bore. It was a straight fashion show. I already dressed pretty swell for a hood dude but I definitely didn't fit in with these squares. Most of them thought of me as a hood already but I shocked them when I challenged them academically. Of course, they placed me in all of the advanced classed because of my intellect, but none of them respected my angle, my understanding of social concepts, or the truth behind the historical information they were trying to teach us. I mean…sure, Shakespeare was one of the most famed writers, authors, and playwrights of his era, but where was his angle on family honor as opposed to love? I didn't believe in true love without God. He came from the Middle Ages; when faith wasn't respected and those who opposed one religion were burned at the stake. His work wasn't compared to anyone else's either. The degree of his literary works was tightly skewed due to his limited audience and had no relation to today's language. White folks only praised his work because of his good use of the English language in a time when that was all they had. Moreover, I didn't buy into the idea of calling civilizations "primitive" when the only separation was unique building structures. I asked the teachers to explain the building of the pyramids without the technological advancement of today and my question stumped them. I always asked these type of questions because I knew if I allowed their lectures to progress, it would result in them calling my neighborhood "less developed" because our beliefs went against some societal norms. I didn't always agree with what went on in the hood, but I would defend it with absolute knowledge and my own self-acquired theories. I didn't agree with what was in their textbooks or what they taught.

 I eventually started to only show up for a couple of classes a day. If people didn't think I was a gangster before they knew about me, they became believers when I took the cops on a high-speed chase through the school neighborhood. It was lunchtime. A couple of my homeboys and I were in my car smoking weed. The cops rolled passed us as we were parked and we tried to not look too obvious. I quickly remembered that I had about two ounces of hard and my gun in the car. When I saw their reverse lights come on, I started up the whip and pulled off. I got about a block away before they busted a U-turn. I was rolling past the front of the school when they started to head my way. The people in the car with me hopped out and I smashed on the gas pedal before they had a chance to pull up behind me and turn their lights on. My tires screeched and caused a huge smoke screen and it gave me a little leeway. Everyone was outside at the time and witnessed this chase. I was not pulling over until I tossed my gun and my work out of the car. I called the only person that I knew at the school with a phone, T. Mini. I called him while doing 60 miles per hour through the residential neighborhood with the cop car on my ass! I told him that I was going to be circling back in 90 seconds and I was going to throw a bag out the window after I hit the corner. He said, "Bet!" I had to drive past the school again to get there but I made it happen. Good thing I chose the spot that I chose because they barricaded the block after the next turn. They kicked my ass a little as they dragged me out of my car. I was booked into juvenile detention and charged with eluding, reckless driving, and possession of marijuana. I wasn't tripping. I knew that I would have *really* gotten broke off if they would have found the gun and the coke. I was there for about a week before they allowed my mom to come pick me up. My public defender said that I was looking at three to six months in detention due to my previous criminal record. I spent the rest of my junior year in the juvenile detention center.

When I got out, I was about three inches taller and about 25 pounds heavier. It was my senior year in high school and I wasn't allowed to attend any Seattle Public Schools because of my antics during my high-speed chase. I had to go to an alternative school and I was fine with it. I went to Marshall Alternative out north. I was cool with it because it gave me a chance to catch up on credits that I lost while I was locked up. I liked the atmosphere at Marshall, anyway. It wasn't all disobedient kids who had been kicked out of other schools. There were a lot of high school moms there that were simply catching up on credits they missed out on because of pregnancy, people who were just trying to get an opportunity to get more credits, and those who just didn't like the traditional high school scene. Furthermore, Marshall Alternative High School didn't have a school weed man. And that's where I found my opportunity. The teachers there were more down to earth. If you came to class late, high, or smelling like weed, they wouldn't say anything unless you caused a disturbance in class.

By this time, my brother, Tyree, was also attending Marshall. After he experienced some misfortune in the dope game, he got into the weed game too. You see, I had been selling dope for about four to five years and never caught a case. However, I did have plenty of close calls. Tyree saw me making money during this time and tried to get into the game by getting some work from one of his friends at school. It worked a few times, but he ended up getting caught by the school security guard and got expelled from the school district, too. It was my fault though. I should have schooled him like Dad schooled me. But shit, I was still soaking up game myself and was caught up in the life. I don't think I could've adequately laced him during that time, but I should've tried. Tyree tried to stay straight and narrow for a minute but ended up getting back into the game, just selling weed. His hustling skills were much more raw than mine. I was schooled by some older cats and often went to them for advice. Tyree just went with the flow and learned as he went along. Sure, he made a bunch of mistakes but never the same ones twice.

    This was the first time that Tyree and I attended the same school at the same time since elementary school. We would wake up in the morning and go to the bus stop together if one of us didn't have a car at the time. We'd usually smoke a couple of blunts on the way to school. We did our thang for a minute. At school, we were simply known as "The Brothers". Other people tried to sell weed at Marshall but they weren't as fly as us. We gave deals, matched blunts, plus, we always had the best weed. Man, did we have fun! Sometimes we'd make more money at school than we did in the streets. People came to Marshall from other schools just to buy weed from us. I still sold dope once I got back to the hood because that shit never slowed up. My heart was embellished in the dope game because that's where I started and it's what I knew best. From that, I learned the imperishable conveniences of putting hustling to all aspects of my character. I sold whatever, whenever, and I learned how to do it carefully. But the weed game was fun. Sure, we were only slanging small weight but we made our dough! We bagged that shit up in dime bags and met profit margins that others weren't making. We could've gotten into buying and slanging pounds back then, but it would've been more risky and nowhere near as fun as slanging dime bags as teenagers.

I remember Tyree and I were walking to school one morning when this older lady pulled up on us with a little girl in the front seat. It was our little sister, Takari, and she was with her grandma. She was so happy to see us! Tyree and I hadn't seen her since she was a baby. She was beautiful! She was dark-skinned just like us and had the cutest little ponytails in her hair. She still had Tyree's round face too. We talked to them for a minute and found out that she attended a private school right up the street from our house. It was a trip to find out she attended a school in our neighborhood and this was our first time seeing her. After my dad went to jail, her mom did her best to keep her away from our side of the family. I heard that Jackie, Ta'Kari's mom, tried to broker a drug deal between my dad and her cousins before he went down. Later, after my dad got locked up, he found out that her cousins were working with the Feds and that Jackie was aware of this. We found it surprising that Takari was still living in Seattle. The last we heard, her mother had married a basketball player who played for the Lakers. We thought she lived down there. But her grandma told us that she lived up here in Seattle with her. We talked for a minute, exchanged numbers, and promised to stay in touch.

"We have numerous fans throughout our lives. We have the ones who vocally tell us how much they admire and appreciate us. We have the ones who cheer for us whenever, however, and are there to tell us how well we've done; even in defeat. Then we have those who believe in us and display a life as a sermon of righteousness for us to witness. These fans are our angels."

The Breakdown

1997 - 1998

We tried our best to be discreet around the house when Grandma was home. We wouldn't smoke weed in the house when she was there and we'd usually meet our joogs around the corner from the house to reduce traffic. She got a whiff of bud from our room once or twice before but she never said anything about it. We kind of figured she charged it to Mom and Craig. She knew what they did. She just didn't say anything because they respected her enough to not cause too much traffic or any activity around the house while she was home. Grandma was a psychologist. She knew all about human behaviors, tendencies, propensities, and characteristics. We knew she had more than just assumptions as to what was going on. She understood how drugs and society worked and that it was affecting all of us. She didn't turn a blind-eye to what was going on. She just made sure that we kept ourselves under control, and no matter what, she made sure that we went to church with her EVERY Sunday. She worked 6-7 days a week and figured that if she had enough time and energy to attend church, there should be no reason why we couldn't make it.

My youngest brother, Craig Jr. (CJ), was born in 1995. He was a smart kid and had one of the funniest personalities. He used to act out lines from the movies he watched all day. I remember I used to take him around with me and people would always think he was my son. We didn't look anything alike. I believe people assumed he was my son because of the age difference and a lot of people my age had a kid already. My mom was still in her addiction but stopped everything after she found out that she was pregnant. People used to say all kinds of shit about him. They'd say that he was going to be a crack baby, slow, or was going to have some kind of birth defect. CJ came out fine. He was actually smarter than a lot of the other kids his age.

One day, we got a phone call from one of Grandma's friends and they told us that Grandma fell or passed out on her way home. They said that she was picked up by an ambulance and taken to the hospital. My mom was at work at a non-profit agency that she recently started working at, so Craig and I were the only ones home when we got the call. We weren't tripping because it didn't sound serious. Craig took the initiative to drive up there to make sure she was alright. I stayed home and kept an eye on CJ. About an hour later, Craig called us from the hospital and told me that Grandma was dead. I didn't believe him at first. I couldn't. I said, "Craig, stop playing. Make sure they have the right name. Those people at the hospital be swamped and get shit mixed a lot." He responded, "Ty, they just handed me her ID and said this lady was brought in and pronounced dead on the way to the hospital." I made my way up to the hospital only to find out that my grandma suffered a massive heart attack on her way home from work. I didn't understand it. She was in good health. I wanted to speak to the doctors and ask them why and how this could've happened? This shit didn't make any sense to me. I spoke to one of the physicians who worked on trying to revive her and he said, "Your grandmother didn't feel any pain. I can guarantee you that she was gone before she hit the floor." I guess he thought these words were comforting? This was shocking to everyone who knew my grandma.

My mother was hurt by losing her mother and couldn't picture going on without her. Tyree distanced himself for a while. They both took different routes in dealing with Grandma's death but they both would inherit strength from it in the future.

I dealt with my grandma's death horribly. Usually, I only drank alcohol on the weekend when I was out kicking it with the homies. We just did it sometimes because we wanted a reason to act more stupid than usual. I started drinking beer with my mother on occasion because it kind of intensified my weed buzz. When Grandma died, I found my solace in alcohol. It helped me mourn. Not that I needed any more help with that. I was grief stricken and I kind of secluded myself. I'd never lost anyone so close to me. When Grandpa Jerome died, I was young. I mean…we were close…but not as close as I was to my grandma. She was the matriarch of our family and the glue that held us together. If there were ever a problem, she would find a way to fix it or give us the encouragement needed to deal with it. This appeared to be the beginning to an end for me. I started drinking more and engaging in behavior that was counterproductive to my hustling. I was already gang-bangin' but I always put my hustle first. My hurt mixed with alcoholic rage caused me to bang harder. It was obvious to all of my friends and family that something was affecting me. I took my grief, anger, and frustration out on my enemies. If I couldn't find any, I would create some. My erratic behavior had a lot of my friends and family members worried about me.

There was a small war going on between the CD and the South End Crips and I was knee-deep in it. Within the next few months, I was questioned in two shootings and arrested for gun possession. I was released on my own personal recognizance due to a lack of evidence. I had to bail out on the pistol charge. I knew it was going to stick because it was in the car that I was driving when I got pulled over. The only chance I had at beating it was claiming an illegal search. While I was awaiting trial, I was still on the streets. A couple of my homies and I were chilling by the park when some cats from the South End snuck up on us. I heard my homie Clown yell, "Squallay!" That was code for us to run. Most of us looked before running. When I looked back I saw about six or seven Crips coming towards us. When they saw us starting to run, they started shooting. I had no time to go and get the gun that I stashed nearby. My homeboy, Craze, was the biggest out of all of us and fell behind. He took a hit in his back. When I saw him drop, I hit a fence that was nearby and ducked behind a car. The Crips got to the fence, turned around, and ran back to where they came from. I was able to see where they went from where I was. My biggest concern was Craze. I wasn't far from him. When I got to him he wasn't moving but he was breathing. When I rolled him over he opened his eyes and started talking. He said, "I was just playing possum in case they tried to come finish me off." He tried to get up and move which was a good sign he wasn't paralyzed. I told him to stay down and wait for the rest of the homies to come pick us up. The police got there before the ambulance or the homies. They tended to Craze but handcuffed me and threw me into the back of the police car.

They brought me back to the police station and questioned me about the shooting. They wanted to know who it was, where they came from, and why they ambushed us? I played dumb as a muthafucka. I told them I didn't know anything. They had me in the box for over three hours and threatened to throw me in a tank that was heavily populated with Crips and other South End gang members. They knew their threats wouldn't faze me. They knew what type of animal I was. I would take off on the biggest one in the tank, probably take a good beating, and PC up until a lawyer from the ACLU came through. They released me and told me they were going to keep a close eye on me.

Craze was cool and didn't suffer any extensive internal damage. He was out of the hospital within two days. The older homies in the hood held a meeting at the same park a week later. The agenda was: payback.

The South End continued to play Genoa City to our Venice. The big homies, BG and Butchie, planned a meeting and recruited some younger homies for retaliation. Butchie was a solidified gangster from Deuce 8. He had been bangin for years and had a lot of influence with the younger G's. BG was a brute from Union. He didn't talk much but he definitely put in work. He played a big part in running the Crips out of the CD a few years back. His name rang bells. A lot of the younger homies were down to ride. This was their opportunity to make a name for themselves. I had plans on riding too. Shit, I was one of the people they were shooting at and they shot my homie Craze. Craze and I were like family. We had been cool for years and he had a baby with my cousin Nikki. I knew if some shit went down and I got hit, he would ride for me. Butchie found out who shot at us, where they were from, and how retaliation was going to be conducted. He formulated a plan to put in motion. Word around the hood was that Butchie was as strategic as they come when it came to planning out gangster shit. I heard one of the homies say a while ago, "Butchie would have made a good military general if he had gone that route."

When the meeting was over, BG and Butchie told me to stay behind to holler at them for a minute. Butchie said, "T, I can't let you ride." I said, "Nigga, I'm riding!" He said, "Look, I got word from your Pops the other day and he said not to let you ride on this one. He's heard about all the heat that's on you and feels you're an emotional wreck since your grandma passed. Your dad is *MY* big homie and he told me to do whatever I had to do to prevent you from riding on this one." I pleaded with him for a minute but he didn't budge. BG, who played more of an enforcer role, stepped in and said, "Little nigga, you're not going! Orders are or-dez." I wasn't arguing with that dude. Butchie spoke more relatively to me and advised me to get back to my hustling. "Cats in the hood need to see that kind of shit going on. It inspires the broke ones", he said to me in a persuasive manner.

I got back to my grind but it was different. First of all, I wasn't selling much weed. I wanted more money so I started pushing more dope for faster profit. Secondly, I started getting some females involved in my hustle. I knew a few chicks that hustled and they liked me. I propositioned them with my charm and told them they could be on a winning team by fucking with TLEE. I had three loyal ones and a couple of flunkies. I had this chick Keela. She was a bonafide hustler who worked in the hottest areas. She knew how to stay under the radar and made money while doing so. She had a lot of love for me and even considered herself my girlfriend. Baby girl had a cold temper and the tendency to cut a bitch if she found out another chick was digging me. I made sure I kept her far away from any of my other chicks. I had this female Tasha, who I met out north while hustling with my cousin Jay. She was a little different. She was hood but a little more business oriented than the other chicks I fucked with. We hustled out of the hotels out north. Tasha would make nice with all of the hotel managers and even cut them in on some of the profits if they let us work out of the rooms. I actually knocked her from one of Jay's homeboys and it caused a little friction. I didn't care. The dude wasn't using her right. If I wanted a chick, I got her. It was a principle I lived by because I had the potential to bring the best out of a chick and make money. Other dudes just wanted to lay up and be "fuck boys" with them or play house. Shit, once I got them singing my "Get This Money" theme song, it was a wrap from there.

    I had this older chick named Sheila who had her own spot. She had a baby by a guy who got sent to the pen a few years back on a murder beef. She was a little overweight but kept herself up. She loved the fact that my young ass was sweet on her. She sold weed for me out of her spot and would call me if any major dope joogs came her way. Dealing with Sheila required a lot of my time and I didn't have it like that. Plus, I wasn't ready to be playing daddy to another man's kid. I was too young and fly for that.

The third difference was that I was becoming a bit of an alcoholic. I was drinking every night. I managed to get my hustle on during the day, but by nightfall, I would have a bottle of cognac waiting for me. I hadn't experienced any blackouts yet, but I was arrested once or twice for being drunk in public and was charged with a DUI from a car accident that I was in. I almost killed myself but I managed to survive by wearing my seatbelt. My pistol case was wrapping up. I agreed to do 6-9 months but was granted the opportunity to do it in work release.

I had a blazing summer and turned myself into work release in the fall. I got a job at my patna Dennis' newspaper company and he knew the deal. Dennis said as long as I did my job, he wouldn't trip. Dennis inherited the newspaper company from his dad. It had become a pretty prominent business in the city over the last few decades. Dennis wasn't a square. He did some time when he was younger and went straight once he got out. He had to. His Pops wouldn't have left him the business if he didn't straighten up his act. He shaped up, got control of the business, and made some prominent changes that helped the business expand. One thing Dennis did, something that I loved, was provide job opportunities for younger brothas in the hood to make some legal money. Everyone didn't wanna sell dope and risk their freedom. Dennis, and other business owners like him, provided job opportunities for people in the hood. I promised Dennis before I started that I wouldn't bring any heat his way. I didn't. As a matter of fact, I never had the opportunity. When I left work release to go to work on the first day, I ran into a couple of my homies, Omar and Crook. I was walking because I wasn't allowed to have a car. They had weed blowing and I hopped in the car with them to get a ride to the newspaper plant. They had some sherm too. Sherm was a hallucinogen that people smoked then. Some people smoked it regularly and others on occasions. I smoked it occasionally because it was fun to trip out, come down, and talk about the experience. I just hit it a couple of times because I had to go to work. It must've been a strong batch because I had a mean trip. I vaguely remember walking through the hood and being on some weird shit. I remember people were trying to talk to me but I couldn't put their words together, so I just nodded my head in agreeance. Last thing I remember was waking up at the baseball dugout by the community center later on that night. The workday was over and it was well past the time I was supposed to report back to work release for the day. I was fucked. I couldn't go back to work release this late. I would've gotten arrested and would've had to finish the rest of my time in jail. I was nowhere near ready to do that shit. So, I was on the run.

We ended up having to move out of the big house about a year after Grandma passed. We couldn't keep up with the mortgage and it ended up getting foreclosed. My mom, Craig, Thomas, and CJ found temporary housing until Mom had the proper resources to acquire permanent housing. My mom and Craig weren't working at the time. Tyree and I helped by providing them with whatever they needed during their transition. Tyree stayed with his patna Dank. They had been tight since elementary and Dank's mom loved Tyree like he was one of her own. I stayed at Grandma Maureen's but I was rarely there because I was still on the run.

I was still pushing dope tough. I was meeting one of my patnas named Jason from the old school, regularly. He was copping a couple ounces every 2-3

days. I knew Jason from way back in my H[o]
days. Even though he was from the South En[d, I]
was from the CD, we remained cool and even [broke]
bread together. When he was locked up, I went [to his]
house and checked up on his mom from time to [time.]
Jason had some dude he called "P" with him one [day]
I met up with him. He said that "P" was his cousi[n]
from Louisiana and that he was hustling with him. I
could say that I didn't like him from the beginning
because I never paid that much attention to how I felt
about him. I just didn't trust him off pure instinct. I
didn't trust anyone from out of state. My philosophy
was that these dudes could kill me and go back home.
Shit, we didn't even know these guy's government
names or the person they were before coming up
here. We had a lot of "out of town" dudes up here
because of hustling opportunities and that good
Seattle weed. I had a few people that I was cool with
and even did business with them, but I never trusted
any of them. However, P started copping with Jason
after a while. I'd serve him but never without Jason
being there. I remember one time they called and
wanted a quarter-bird. I wasn't pushing that type of
weight so I had my connect front it to me, and
everything went cool. We did this a couple of times
before P called me up by himself one day. I went to
meet him with my homie Craze. I was trying to get
him incorporated in this dope game because by then
he had another mouth to feed and had trouble finding
a steady job. Plus, I needed his muscle. When I went
to meet P, something seemed fishy. He didn't have
Jason with him and he wasn't in his car. That was the
first red flag. The second red flag was that he was
riding with this dude named Train. Train was another
dude that I knew from the old school. We had a
minor beef a little while ago. We had gotten over it
but we still didn't like each other. I hopped out of the

car and dropped the bag of goods on the ground and asked, "Where's the chips?" P hopped out and so did Train, except Train flashed a burner. As Train went to slide the hammer back on his pistol, I swung to punch him and almost missed him. I saw P pull out a gun too, so I took off running. They started shooting at me but I didn't slow down a bit. As I hopped a fence, I felt a sharp pain in my ass but it wasn't painful enough to break my stride. I glimpsed back as I was running and saw that Craze was still there tussling with Train over the bag of goods. I finally stopped running after I didn't hear any more shots. About twenty seconds later, I heard two more shots. I knew Craze was the type of person to try to fight them off. He wouldn't have given up the coke because someone flashed a burner. Those two shots were probably the last thing he would ever hear. I could hear police sirens nearing as I started to head back to the scene. So, I ducked off into a cab and bounced. The pain I felt in my ass had grown stronger and was traveling up my back as I rode in the cab. I reached back and there was blood on the seat. I had been shot.

    I went to the hospital to get treated for my gun wound. I had no idea that I was shot. I guess all of the adrenaline rushing through me as I was running had an impact on me? Of course, the police came to interview me. They wanted to know what happened. I was shot, Craze was dead, and his body was lying by a vehicle that I was known to drive. I told them that Craze and I were chilling and were ambushed by some cats trying to rob us. They wanted to know who they were. I told them I didn't know? I didn't tell them who it was because if they got arrested, it would fuck up any revenge me and my niggas were planning. Plus, if I did tell who it was, people would call me a snitch and it might fuck up my business and ruin my reputation. Gangsters didn't snitch. When somebody did something to us or one of our peoples, we handled our business and retaliated. We didn't get the cops involved. Craze's mom was heated. His brother was too, but he understood. He knew the game. He also knew we would take care of shit.

    The bullet went up and lodged in my back, near my spine. The doctors said it would cause more damage removing it than it would by just leaving it in there. The police pressured me the whole time I was at the hospital. They tried to use the fact that I had an active warrant for not reporting to work release as their leverage. They knew I wasn't trying to go to jail in my condition. They kept bringing me an array of photos of possible suspects, so I acted like cats looked familiar just to string them along and use it as leverage for myself. Then Detective Lundbar came in. He was the lead detective of the gang unit and monitored drug activity because it related to gang activity. We had some previous run-ins on the streets because of my recent episodes. Apparently, Lundbar had been keeping an eye on me. He said that he knew about the moves I've been making, some of my main connects, my gangster lifestyle, and even the females I've been fucking with. I acted like I didn't understand what he was talking about but he knew that I did. Lundbar was known for being aggressive and persuasive during his line of questioning but he made it clear that all he wanted was P. I learned P's real name was Percy DuBois. He was up here from Louisiana because he was wanted in connection to a murder and a number of other felonies in New Orleans. Lundbar spoke in a demanding, yet, calm tone and said, "Tyrome, I can hold you in jail until you tell me everything that I need to know. Then after that, I can continue to hold you until trial starts and you give the testimony that I need to convict the people who shot you and killed Craze. Only after that will you start doing your time for your existing legal problems and whatever else I can make stick." I have to admit I was rattled. It seemed like a long time to be in county jail. I knew I couldn't be there as a witness to a murder being prepped to testify. I wouldn't last. Lundbar continued, "But you know what? I want this guy Percy more than you know. I'm going to have a patrol car stake your grandma's house until you heal. We'll come back and speak to you in a couple of days and get your statement." This was my break.

"One can never appreciate the discomfort of his own tormented life without experiencing someone else's tormented reality. Our luxuries are considered as such by others and we have the opportunity to deal with the issues we created from what society has given us. In all actuality, the presence of violence, inequalities, and oppressive systems were present before we made it here to America. Identifying them only made those who possessed privilege, ready to expound on them; and the other group forever coping with their existence."

The Greater Antilles

1998 - 1999

Lundbar was on my ass. He was at my grandma's house every other day questioning me about the shooting. He knew P shot me but I just wouldn't come out and say it. I went over what happened during the incident numerous times but he noticed the discrepancies every time I told him. I either left something out, was inconsistent with describing the way the crime scene was laid out, or went against forensic evidence. Finally he said, "Look, Tyrome, I'm going to go back to my office and put together all of your statements into one. When I get back, you're going to read over it and sign it, acknowledging Percy was the one who shot you and your friend. If you don't, or have any more changes to make, or recant in any way, I'm arresting you on your warrants and charging you with "Leaving the Scene of a Crime". Then he left. He didn't even wait for me to agree or disagree with it. I sat there and rambled with my thoughts around the situation. I weighed the differences in the circumstances of agreeing to sign the statement, testifying, and dealing with the repercussions from that.

    I thought about what would happen if I didn't sign, refused to testify, and spent months or maybe even a year in jail, protecting the identity of the person who robbed me, and killed my patna. I went upstairs to talk to my grandma about it. I told her the circumstances and the options I had. Grandma Maureen wasn't a college educated, Christian woman with a PhD in psychology like Grandma Johnnie. Nope. She was a Catholic-raised, Trinidadian woman with an eighth grade education. She wasn't big on religion but she was a realist. She listened to me as I told her my circumstances. She knew that no matter what, I was going to have to go back to the hood eventually because my momma was there. She knew how us Lee boys were crazy about our mommas. She also didn't want to see any more of her kids in prison, and if she could do anything to prevent that, she would. Grandma made a couple of phone calls to some friends of hers, but it was weird. Grandma had been in America nearly all of her life so she spoke with a very slight accent. I mean…you would only notice it if you paid attention to certain words or if you had just met her. I heard her talking on the phone and she was speaking a language I've never heard her speak before. When she hung up she said, "Go pack a bag. Your aunt will be here in 20 minutes." Grandma Maureen and Auntie Vernice got me a passport together. Grandma spoke with my grandpa's sister down in Jamaica to arrange for me to come down there for a little while. She figured that I could enjoy myself down there while I waited for the heat to die down or for Detective Lundbar to build his case without me. I never knew my grandpa had siblings because he never talked about them. I just knew he left Jamaica at an early age and came to America. I used a passport and an ID that my aunt Vernice made for me to get down there.

    I was supposed to meet three of my cousins at the airport. My grandma told me that my cousin Janky would be picking me up. I didn't know who or what to look for. I wandered around the outside of the airport for a half an hour before he found me. This tall, lanky, bald-headed man walked up to me and said with a heavy accent, "Yamus be Lil Ty?" I replied, "Janky?" He said, "Ya know it! Wer ya wanderin to?" Honestly, I couldn't understand half of his lingo but it sounded like he was agreeing to who he was. We walked to his car, which was a beat up station wagon. We hopped into the car with two other people who were also my cousins. Their names were Gerald and Peetey. After the introductions, we started riding and conversing but it was hard for me to understand them. Halfway through the ride I said, "Look, you guys are going to have to slow down or speak more clearly because I can't understand half of what ya'll saying." They laughed out loud and then Peety said, "That's good! We finit difficult to cam prehen ya words too!" I laughed with them. Janky said, "Don't war bout dat. Will get use ta each otha soon." This was comforting but I knew I was in for some culture shock.

When we got the house where Janky lived, I was tripping. This was nothing like I had imagined. This was the point when I realized I wasn't in the hood anymore. They lived in what looked like a rundown apartment building. The building looked dilapidated from the outside, but the insides where plushed out. Janky's mom, Jeanie, was my grandpa's oldest sister. She stood about 6'2" and she walked with a slight limp. She was dark-skinned, with long gray dreadlocks, and she had blue eyes. I'd never seen that before. I said, "You must be my Great Auntie Jeanie?" She replied with a great big smile, exposing multiple missing teeth, "Yamus be me great nephew?" I gave her a hug and we inside her house.

Aunt Jeanie and I talked for hours. Her, my cousins, and I smoked some of the fattest joints that I've ever puffed on! And I ate some of the spiciest food known to man! The shit had my mouth burning for hours! I met a bunch of my other relatives that also lived in the neighborhood. Actually, they didn't call them neighborhoods. They called them "garrisons". My cousins lived in a garrison named "Tivoli Gardens". It was real hype around that time because of who was in power politically. P.J. Peterson was Prime Minister of Jamaica at that time, meaning the People's National Party (PNP) was in control. But I soon learned that the Jamaican Labour Party (JLP) had a lot to say about that. My cousins seemed happy to see me but they kept asking me why I came and how long was I going to stay? I gave them vague answers because my grandma told me not to let them know why I was there. She didn't necessarily tell me to not tell anybody. She just said that it might not be a good idea.

My cousins ran around smoking weed, chasing girls, and playing soccer all day. Some of them had jobs and others were part of the local gangs that fought against the JLP in the nearby garrisons. These guys didn't have beef that was equivalent to what the Crips and Bloods had in America. These cats were at war with the people who literally lived across the street. There was a huge brush of bushes that separated the east side of the Tivoli Gardens from the west end. The JLP gang mostly occupied that small portion. Most of the fighting occurred during the night. It would be dark as hell but you would see flashes of bullets zipping through the bushes. It seemed like someone got hit every night. We actually lost one of my younger cousins while I was there. I tried to stay out of that mess as much as I could. I'd usually be in the house chilling with my aunt.

My aunt told me a lot more about my grandpa and my family history. I learned some interesting things about Jamaica's history and some of the first inhabitants of the island. Actually, our family wasn't originally from Jamaica. My great-great-grandparents came over from Haiti. I learned that I had some revolutionary roots in my blood and that my ancestors were the Jamaican Maroons. My aunt informed me that we were descendants of Louveture Toussaint; the great liberator of Haiti. He was the Black general who defeated Napoleon's French army and made Haiti the first all-Black governed country in the world.

Aunt Jeanine had a sister named Ophelia. My aunt Jeanie had a big fight with Ophelia and her brother years ago and Ophelia moved to Montego Bay with her husband and kids. Aunt Jeanie said she hadn't spoken to her in nearly twenty years. She said that their brother, Samuel, died shortly after Ophelia left. He was killed in a war between Tivoli and Olympic Gardens, leaving Aunt Jeanie to raise his kids. She said that her father, my great-grandpa James, lived to be eighty-five and his wife, my great-grandma Victoria, lived to be ninety-seven. She had pictures, drawings, and other family heirlooms that had been passed down for generations. I felt proud to get all of this knowledge about my family history. Here I was, just thinking that my grandpa was a regular dude, not knowing the origins of his roots, or the genetic strengths he passed down to us. I was amazed to learn about my ancestry. I'm sure that I'm not the only one who figured that their family ancestry was lost due to slavery, oppression, and hardship. I felt proud to know that I had such a rich ancestry. I was thankful to learn this.

I had been in Jamaica for a little over a month. The beautiful people, the beaches, and the laze-faire lifestyle that the inhabitants enjoyed intrigued me. The beach life was amazing! But less than a mile inward from the beaches were the garrisons. They don't tell you about that shit in the brochures. That's where all of the mayhem took place. It was cool for the main part of the day when people were out working and handling their daily business. But when nightfall hit the poverty infested dirt roads of the garrisons, it turned into a warzone. I don't think there was a night that I was there in which I didn't hear gunshots or witness some bizarre rumble that usually left someone mortally wounded. But I loved Jamaica!

I loved seeing the land, meeting new family, and exploring a totally different culture. I especially enjoyed spending time with my aunt. But I had grown tired of the concentrated battles between the townsmen.

I remember it was like 5 o'clock in the morning when my aunt Jeanie aggressively woke me out of my sleep. I slept upstairs because they were shooting near the house and a bullet shot one of the windows out. It scared the shit out of me! It took me hours to fall asleep afterwards. My aunt woke me up and said, "Nephew, get up! Ya have to go now!" I was still woozy and confused from being awoken so abruptly. I said, "Why? What happened? What did I do?" She said, "Every-ting. Go to da motel Casablanca on da norf end of da beach. A man'll be waitin in room 17-C. I'll be comin soon." Her reason for getting me up so early in the morning was because it was the only time of the day I could travel through the neighboring garrisons with little risk of being harmed.

When I got to the Casablanca, a little dude named Sampson was waiting for me. I said, "What's up? My aunt sent me here. She's supposed to meet me here later." Sampson said, "So you da supa star, yeah?" I said, "What?" Sampson smiled and replied, "Yeah, we saw you on da tee-vee. You da 'Merican on da run, right?" I had a blank stare on my face and thought to myself, "That explains everything." Sampson saw the worry on my face and said, "Don't wary mon'. Ya in good hands, see. Ya aunt was good ta-me wen I needed."

Aunt Jeanie came to the room later that day. She informed me that while the police were searching for another American fugitive hiding in Jamaica, they found out I was there, too. There was a reward for the other fugitive so a lot of people figured that there must've been a reward for my capture, as well. She said that some people were planning on tying me up and turning me in to the authorities. I said, "But Auntie, I'm around family all day. They wouldn't let anyone do anything to me." Aunt Jeanie scooted a little closer, looked me dead in my eyes, and said, "Who da ya tink was doin the plottin?" I thought that I was fucked at that point. Even family was turning against me? I couldn't really blame them. They didn't know me like that. If I were living in the kind of poverty they were living in, I might've turned in a newly met, distant cousin for a bag of cash too. I knew I had to get up out of there. Aunt Jeanie said she was going to find a secure phone so I could call to let my grandma know the trouble that I was in. I asked my aunt if she could give me a couple of bucks to get some food. I left the little money that I had at her house because I had to get out of the house so quickly. She spotted me a couple of bucks and said she would be back in an hour.

I waited until my Aunt Jeanie was gone for about ten minutes before I made my move. My hair was in two French-braids. I took them out and put all of my hair into one ponytail and then put on a hat. Outside of the hotel were a couple of taxis. I hopped into one of them and said in my best Jamaican accent, "Take me toda 'merican embassy." I got to the embassy and walked to the gate and said, "My name is Tyrome Lee. I am an American citizen and a fugitive on the run." They let me in immediately. I heard one of the embassy guards utter to another, "The townspeople must've found out he was a fugitive."

As soon as I stepped foot onto American soil, I was immediately arrested. I was charged with a number of felonies. But I had a public defender get my escape charges dropped due to the fact that I was never in custody. I plead to a bunch of lesser charges in return for my testimony. I had no choice in the matter. I had to take the stand no matter what. But what I said once I got up there was a totally different story. I had to condition my mind to believe that I wasn't testifying against any of my homies. Instead, I forced myself into believing that I was letting 12 strangers know who robbed and shot me, and killed my cousin's baby's daddy while we were unarmed. If I didn't "agree" to testify and went to trial for my charges and lost, I would've got somewhere between 5-7 years in prison. I took 14 months with credit for 5 months, without a question.

But luck jumped on my side! During the time that I was gone, the prosecution gathered some forensic evidence against P, and they tried to use it to get him to squeeze on Train. He refused to tell on him. P and Train knew that I was on the run because I didn't want to testify. When P heard that I was captured and was offered a deal that included me testifying, he started shopping a deal. I only agreed to say that P shot me. I told them that I didn't know who Train was or who killed Craze. I did this because I knew Train and had plans on handling him later and in a different way. P ended up pleading to second-degree murder and was sentenced to 20 years. He never told on Train. Not because he was a stand up dude; but because he wasn't from here and Train had tons of peoples in our state's penal system. He would've never survived if he did. I got to keep my deal without testifying. Train gave me 10 thousand dollars as a gesture but I assumed that it was for my troubles and not fingering him. I gave it to Craze's mom and his baby's mom. I served 8 months. Train was killed in a car accident 4 months later.

> *"You can only tame an animal if you put in the time and create an environment for it to internalize the complete understanding of who is in control. If the animal is a natural predator, it will use the same tactics amongst other inhabitants within its domain. It's an animalistic, sociological formality that trickles down the power dynamics."*

Back At It

1999 - 2001

When I got out I hopped right back in the game. I wasn't selling dope as much because I knew how much time I could get for a simple possession. So, I started slanging weed on a whole different scale. Yeah, I still sold bags but I primarily sold weight. Tyree was in the weed game tough too, but he also sold dope. We had a weed connect that only fucked with us. I was a solo act. I mean…I fucked with cats and socialized regularly but I hustled by myself. Tyree had a crew he hustled with. They were cats that he had known for a while and he trusted these dudes. Dank was big Black kid who was as loyal as they came. Him and Tyree were super close and did a lot of dirt together. Dank was the only person Tyree completely trusted other than me. They were more like brothers. They called each other's mom "Mom", shared clothes, and did everything together. By this time, Tyree had grown bigger than me. He didn't ever try to throw his size around on me but I definitely wasn't gonna try to physically force him to do anything. It would've been an uphill battle and I would've had to use all power, skill, and expertise to do so. I was good with being respected as his big brother.

Tyree and Dank had a White buddy named Wolf who they kept close. Wolf didn't gang-bang, sell drugs, or get involved in violence like them. Tyree brought Wolf home on his way home from school one day. He came into the house and everyone said, "Hey Tyree, who's the White guy?" Tyree said, "Oh, that's my new friend, Wolf. He smokes weed." That was all that needed to be said. He started hanging out with us almost every day. Wolf was a rebellious, defiant kid. He came from a middle-class Jewish family but hated the traditional family structure. He just felt like he fit in with us more and we had no problem with it. He kept it real with us and didn't try to be anyone he wasn't. Wolf dibbled and dabbled in the weed game but nothing too heavy. He had us running a check-cashing scheme for a minute but we gave it up when a couple of our homies got broke off with some major fed time behind it. Then there was 50; a straight up hustler. 50 used to cop work from me when he was younger and he grew tight with Tyree when they used to hit the blade together. He'd been locked up a few times for slanging but was true to the turf. He wasn't as goofy as Tyree and Dank. He was a little quieter and didn't really fuck around. A couple of people looked at his anti-social behavior as a weakness and tried to test him. While I was locked up, I heard that a couple of dudes from the hood robbed him. He didn't tell anyone what happened. They found one of the guys dead in the park and the other dude got shot up two days later. Nobody really knew what happened to them and people didn't hear from 50 for about a month. He came back the same dude and didn't really speak to anyone about it except for Tyree. Shit, he wouldn't even tell me! I just knew that if he had my brother's trust, then he had mine.

    Tyree and his crew built up a little rep for themselves. They were known for having an extensive grind and not putting up with a lot of shit. A lot of other young cats wanted to be down with them and Tyree never refused. He just wouldn't make any of them official members. Yeah, he'd let them cop, hang out, and smoke some bud at one of their spots. But he would never let them cop at wholesale prices or take any of them with him when he met with the connect. Tyree considered me as part of his crew. He felt that I had just as much stock in it as he did because we all mostly hung out together unless I went out to a club, bar, or was laid up with a broad. I liked the solo gig. I didn't have anything against any of them or their hustle. I just didn't like the idea of relying on anyone else when it came to my hustle. Plus, these little goons were animals! They would publicly put the beat down on people that disrespected their grind, their crew, and people they just didn't like. Seattle's street grind wasn't like the east coast where it was more territorial. We didn't battle or beef over blocks. We weren't that greasy. We just let the hustle do the talking and had a lot of competition in the streets. Whoever had the best, or the most work, survived in the streets and made the most money. You had to be able to give deals and compete with others. We learned that in the capitalist market, it wasn't who could sell the product at the highest price. It was who could sell it at the fastest rate while still profiting. It was all about the re-up. The more you ran back to cop from your connect, the stronger the relationship was with him. Doing this strengthened your hustle in a variety of other ways.

We were hustling strong as the new millennium approached. A lot of shit went down at the end of the year that caused some major dysfunction in our grind. First of all, people were getting killed. One night, our connect came home to some guys robbing his house and was murdered. This was crazy because we were pretty close with the connect. His name was Mack and he was cool with our dad back in the day. The fucked up thing about it was that only a couple of people knew where Mack lived; Tyree and I were one of them. Some people started making accusations towards us because of the dealings we had with a bunch of other people in the past. We robbed a few dudes before but they were all off-brand cats that weren't connected to any crew, clique, or gang. We didn't kill anyone either. We just smacked a few of them around while we took their shit. A message had gotten back to Mack's people that we may have had something to do with him being murdered or that we might've known something. I honestly didn't know who put that there. We actually didn't find out about the rumor until Mack's brother, Sherrill, rode up on us one night on the blade with three of his henchmen. We've heard about Sherrill and his doings. We knew this wasn't a regular house visit. Sherrill walked up to us and said, "What ya'll know about my brother getting killed?" Tyree said, "We don't know shit!" This was true. We didn't know anything. We hadn't heard any details about who might've been involved or anyone who knew anything. Sherrill looked at us with an angry, puzzled look on his face. It seemed like he didn't want to believe us. So, he took an aggressive approach in order to get the desired response. He said, "Well niggas is saying you guys might've had a part in this and I think it's ya'll job to convince me you didn't." My thoughts on responding were mixed because I didn't want to say the wrong thing. We honestly didn't want any beef with him. We were considered as goons but not soldiers. Based on that fact alone, I knew we couldn't go to war with this dude. He was older, had more money, and a lot more soldiers on his side than we did. We were known for putting in work. But Sherrill and his crew were known for having people exterminated.

We could see that Sherrill and his men were armed. Our guns were at least 10-15 yards from us. Something came over Tyree. He didn't wait more than two seconds to respond to Sherrill's question. Tyree said, "Nigga we ain't gotta convince shit to you. We hurting too! Mack was our big homie and a good friend of our Pops. How could killing him benefit us? You see we still on the block like we were before that shit happened!" I chimed in and started to say something to ease the way Tyree's words were interpreted but he continued talking. He continued, "Sherrill, you know us, what we're about, and how we get down. You know we don't associate ourselves in that kind of shady business. You could've called us and had a proper meeting and discussed anything regarding this issue. But you run up on us on the block strapped and accuse us in front of people? I feel disrespected." Sherrill was furious but he also felt stupid. He definitely didn't expect a response like that from a young dude. But at the same time, he respected his realness. He asked Tyree, "Where do you get balls to talk to me like that?" This was a test. If Tyree would've responded without the same sincerity and aggression, there's no telling where this altercation might've went. My little brother quickly responded, "Where do you get the nerve to come accusing some real dudes of some bullshit based on rumors?" Sherrill said, "Alright, I'm gonna ask around a little more but I'll be back." Tyree said,

"We'll be right here." And then they left. I started to scold Tyree about how he responded to them. I said, "Man, what the fuck is wrong with you talking to them like that?!" Tyree said, "Oh! What?! Now you gonna get mad at me for keeping it real? Come on, Ty. You taught me better than that."

    We were rattled for a while after that confrontation. We had a few other spots we slanged out of and crashed at sometimes but they were too hot for us to stay longer than a day or two. We stayed at Mom's house for the most part. We slept with our pistols loaded by our bedside for the next several days. I started drinking more and we were all popping ecstasy pills on a daily basis around this time. Ecstasy usually intensified however we were feeling at the time. Either I would turn into a super pimp, super mack, super gangster; or I would end up fucking the "dog-shit" out of some poor girl who had intentions of making love.

    Tyree and I started asking around and did our own investigation to find out what happened to Mack. When we found out, we got with Sherrill and told him what the deal was. Apparently, Mack had gotten over on some people in California a while back. They found out he was up in Seattle living large and decided to come up here and plot on him. Originally, they just planned on robbing his house but he came home during the robbery. This made killing him a moot point. After we identified who the culprits were, we told Sherrill. He did his own investigating and found the information we came up with was true. Sherrill thanked us for finding out who had a part in killing his brother. He also said, "Hopefully there's no hard feelings about our confrontation a couple of weeks ago? But I was just hurting and following any and all leads. I respect that you and your brother kept it real." I said, "Don't worry about it. We understand. Just call us if you need help with handling that." Sherrill said, "Thanks, but we got this, young blood. They gonna feel this!"

A few weeks later, Tyree got himself into some mess. He had been fronting work to his homeboy Paul but had some issues getting the money out of him. Tyree didn't know at the time that Paul started smoking and that was the reason why he was always coming up short. When Tyree went to confront him, Paul got loud and defensive and they started to scuffle. Tyree pulled out his gun because he didn't want it to go off while they fought; not to try to shoot him. Paul thought otherwise, so he went for the gun. It went off during the struggle and Paul was shot in the back.

When Paul got to the hospital, he told the police what happened and that Tyree was the one who shot him. Tyree went to visit him a couple of days later without knowing that Paul had already told the cops what happened. Tyree was arrested on attempted murder charges and held without bail. I got his crew together to figure out how we were going to handle the situation but Tyree said that he didn't want us to retaliate. He felt bad about accidently shooting Paul, but felt even worse after he found out that he was paralyzed from the waist down. He and Paul were good friends and the whole situation had him fucked up. Tyree was only 17 and was being charged as a juvenile. He knew he could get 4 years if he blew trial but felt like he had action at a plea bargain. Tyree's defense was that it was an accident and he didn't mean to shoot Paul. He wrote a sympathetic letter to the judge stating how bad he felt. He further explained that he and Paul were good friends before the incident. He ended up pleading to assault and a pistol charge. He received 9 months in juvenile.

    While Tyree was gone, his crew didn't do much hustling. They just made enough money to keep their heads afloat due to all of the beefs they were involved in. Dank became territorial and didn't want people who weren't copping from him or his patnas on the block. He exercised this by force. This caused some cats to retaliate in a similar manner. 50 was there but he was more in tune with his girl. She was pregnant with his son and she needed him to be there more. 50 did a lot of time in juvenile and didn't want to risk missing his son being born. He still hustled and put in work when needed, but he chose to play a smaller role in things and only got involved when it was absolutely necessary.

    I met this chick named Alicia through my homeboy Resins. She was a good friend of Resins's girlfriend and we hit it off pretty quickly. We had only been messing around for a few months before she got pregnant. She was good looking and I was probably smitten by her looks more than anything else. I knew Alicia from around the neighborhood but I really didn't have any interest in her in the past. I took a liking to her now because she grew up a lot and hadn't been with a lot of dudes before. A lot of the girls in the hood were run through. If they weren't, it was because they were ugly, horrifically out of shape, or didn't have potential or intangibles that a hood nigga could work with. Alicia looked good and "sounded" smart. She talked a lot about God and religion but I never paid attention to any of it. Mainly, because she talked about that shit all day, but sinned fruitfully in my bedroom at night. I rarely trusted people who constantly quoted Bible verses and talked about God all of the time. Shit, I knew that the Devil knew the Bible back and forth; but God still kicked him out of heaven because he was a "cheap" angel. Alicia's rants about God kind of annoyed me. But she had ass though...

By this time, I had become a full-blown alcoholic and didn't even recognize it. I had always been a pothead. I had been smoking weed daily since I was a teenager. When I was in my late teens, I started drinking occasionally and on weekends, but my drinking intensified after Grandma Johnnie passed. Before I knew it, I was drinking beer daily and buying bottles of Hennessy 3-4 times a week. I felt like I was cool because I hustled daily, had a little money in my pocket, and enough money to get myself out of a jam if needed. I didn't see what was happening to me, or the pain that I caused other people.

I was happy to be having a son! I already planned to name him after me to keep this "T. Lee" shit going. Alicia had a problem with it, of course, but I stayed adamant about it. By the time he was born, my alcoholism had grown worse. I was drinking daily and it was affecting other areas of my life. I had a lot of struggles going on at the same time and not enough sanity to cope. I got Alicia and I an apartment together out south. She wasn't working so I was the sole provider for her and my son. This was cool but she was very unappreciative. I did everything to provide for them and all she did was complain. My hustle was being affected and the game was drying up on me. I was spending so much time with my newborn son that I actually lost a lot of clientele. I was mainly just slanging weed but I wasn't slanging it fast enough to meet all my needs. So, I robbed a few people. I didn't rob any major figures in the game. I just robbed some squares that were trying to come from the suburbs and get into the game without paying their dues. These were mainly White boys who were only in the game to gain some sort of street cred. This helped me stay afloat a few times but I started to build a reputation and a few people stopped doing business with me.

Tyree got out of jail and had his son right after I had mine. He named his son after him, too. Tyree hopped right back in the game and found us a new weed connect from Canada. He was getting weed at a cheaper price than we ever had. This was beneficial because we could lower the price and take out the competition. Tyree had a genius idea though. Our weed was better than everyone else's. His idea was to jack up the price after one week of flooding the streets. The plan was to give people a taste of some good bud and then jack up the price according to its potency. I didn't know that he only planned to lower the price if we sold it in bulk. This made a lot of sense. Sell the little shit for a high price and the weight for cheaper. It made the lower level dealers compete with each other while we raked in the profits based on the potency of our bud. They knew that in order to compete they would have to have the best product. I was a part of Tyree's crew but I laid back and away from the front. I did this because I was getting a little older, wanted to spend time with my son, and because of my alcoholism. As much as Tyree wanted me to help him run shit, I felt he was too out in the open for me. I had a record and didn't wanna go back to jail. I just made my small time joogs to keep the bills paid. I never realized this, but around this time, I was experiencing depression. I was unhappy in my relationship, suffering from alcoholism, and I knew I wasn't living up to my potential. I knew that I was smarter than most people and could create an opportunity to live a much better life. I felt trapped in the game. Either I was going to be happy with the way things were, or take the necessary risks to improve things and risk the chance of going back to jail. I was beneath complacency.

    My Uncle Tommy had just gotten out of prison again. He'd been in and out of prison for the last decade. I swear this guy had a membership there. He came home and was kind of impressed by what he heard about Tyree and I through the prison chatter. Uncle Tommy played a strong influence in our lives even though he would be gone for 3-4 year stretches at a time. To us, he represented absolute realness. He was always true to himself and the core principles of being a Gangster Disciple. Sitting down and talking to him was always inspiring. Uncle Tommy used to tell us stories about our father and other family members that were phenomenal. He always expounded on the miraculous adventures of his father and his brothers. He was the first one in our family to make us feel proud to be a Lee and what that actually meant. They called him T.O. in the streets and he was as gangster and street as they came. If you just looked at him as a gangster, then you'd be stumped by his intelligence. Uncle Tommy used the time he spent in prison to educate himself. I admired him for that. Yeah, he was our uncle and we respected him as that. But he was also our peer who we could relate to and learn from. Uncle Tommy was always in the streets with us whenever he was out. He shared special and unique bonds with Tyree and I. My bond with him stemmed back from my childhood and all of the time we spent together. I could ask Uncle Tommy anything and he would have a reasonable answer for me. He didn't play my father's role but he definitely showed me some things my father missed out on showing me. He and Tyree were both the younger brothers and they connected off of that concept alone. They were both "fat asses" who loved to eat, smoke weed, play video games, and talk shit. I would say that he and Tyree's bond was closer, but that would be saying I didn't value the importance of the bond that him and I had. But those fat fuckers definitely had more fun!

"Who is the real fool? Is it the person who is obviously foolish by all accounts? Or is it the person who accompanies the fool in their foolish nature? Can we agree that everyone plays the part of the fool at certain times, but we never knowingly, play the part of the other? It's better to remain humble and be thought of as a fool, than to display your foolish ways and remove all doubt."

Mike Huntly

2000 - 2003

Alicia had a close friend that she had been cool with for years. Her name was Erica and they were more like sisters. I've known Erica for a while too. She went to middle school with Tyree and she stayed on Union when I first started hustling up that way. I remember after Lil Ty was born, Erica started messing with a dude name Mike. I knew Mike from around town. He was one of those "cheesy" muthafuckas who was known for doing stupid shit. He wasn't a banger or from any hood in particular but he said he claimed Horton Block. Horton was a small neighborhood out south but it was more of a neutral territory. I had a few homies from there and they never claimed allegiance to the CD or South End. They were mostly comprised of G's and a few cats that claimed Crip. Mike lived out south and went to school in the CD, so most people considered him a neutral. We ended up hanging out because Alicia and Erica hung out a lot. Mike drank and smoked weed so we got along for the most part. When I first started hanging with him, Tyree said, "You hanging with Mike Huntley? Man, I heard he was smoking crack not too long ago." I asked Mike about it and he denied it but said, "Naw. I snorted some coke before. But that was it." I didn't think anything of it at that time.

Lil Ty was getting bigger and was learning quickly. He was already walking and he wasn't even a year old yet. Alicia and I were on better terms because I got her involved in the game a little. She said she hated being home alone all day with no visitors. I've never liked letting people know where I lived but I was getting some clientele at my apartment building where we lived. While I was out and about, I had her slang a little bud from the spot.

I hooked up with my Aunt Vernice doing some bank scams and it was highly profitable. Alicia's friend, Erica, was down for whatever and had a versatile look to her that made it possible for her to change her appearance whenever. She was able to go into the bank and successfully cash several checks under different identities. This brought us a couple thousand dollars each time. We were comfortable for the time being. The easy money led to me getting lazy in my hustle. You see…throughout my life, I always put my hustle first. A strong hustle meant that I could provide for my family and I. I never got so lazy that I slowed up on hustling and missing out on joogs. It contributed to my work ethic. But I was drinking heavily and got complacent. The money Erica was making at the time was helping me out while I was in this position.

I found myself hanging out with Mike more since Erica and Alicia were spending more time together. I was a sleaze bag and I knew it. There were times while I was out hustling that I would run into chicks that were diggin me, or ones that I had a thing for. I fooled around a lot but I never got caught because I usually made it home at night. If I didn't, I had a good excuse on why I didn't. It pissed Alicia off every time. She would be mad at me for days and wouldn't talk to me or let me touch her. This would cause me to be out of the house even more because I didn't want to be around her while she was in a bad mood over something I had done days ago. I didn't see all of the pain that I was causing her and she didn't realize that her attitude towards my behavior was counter-productive. But this guy Mike was an economy-size sleaze bag! I'm not saying this because he messed around on Erica heavily; it was the types of females that he messed around on her with. I mean…he'd pick up some of the ugliest, nastiest, trifling-looking women! I passed on a lot of pussy he tried to throw my way. There were times when I would play the wingman, and other times I'd chill at a local bar or something until he was done with one of his mud-ducks. Mike's biggest problem was that he could never cover up his tracks well and was a horrible liar. Erica would always catch him in a lie and they'd go through it. I always tried to tell him to stick to his story and quit making up shit as he went along. I only advised him of this because of the guy code. I was much more loyal to Erica because I'd known her a lot longer. She became more like a little sister to me since I had been with Alicia. But Mike had dirt on me too. So I was obligated to show him some kind of loyalty.

I knew I was a boss. No one had to tell me that. I had been feeling inadequate more often. I felt like I wasn't where I should be in life. My hustle slowed down and so did the money that Erica was making. Alicia and I moved to a different apartment because we had blown up the spot at our previous building. My homeboy, Boog, came to help me move. Boog was another patna of mine that I grew up with. He was from the town but lived out south before moving to the CD. We accepted him in the hood but there were a few cats that didn't like him because they thought he was a part of a South End gang. A lot of cats in the South End didn't like him because they felt like he switched sides. I knew him from the old school, before any of us even started "set trippin". Boog and I did some time together not too long ago. We had to have each other's back against some Tacoma dudes. In the joint, it wasn't about what part of town you were from. It was "the town" against other towns. This was the only place where South End and CD hoods linked up. We kept in contact after we got out and hung out with each other from time to time.

After we moved all of the stuff from my apartment into my new spot, I took Boog and Mike to a bar to hang out and drink. Mike and Boog already knew each other. I didn't know they had minor beef years before, but they squashed it before things got out of hand. They were cool now.

I was at home one night chilling with Alicia and Lil Ty when she got a phone call. Erica called Alicia and was hysterical! She said that she was approached by my cousin, Princess, while she was out. She said Princess told her that she and Mike had been together and that he was her man now. Erica said that when she went to confront Mike about it, he denied it and then started beating on her. She said he was still there drunk and wouldn't leave. Alicia begged me to go over there and do something, but I chose to stay out of it. After Alicia begged and pleaded for another 30 minutes, I decided to drive over there to see what the fuss was. I thought to myself, "It can't be that bad." Erica was a big exaggerator and Mike wasn't a big enough guy to have done too much damage. I figured she might have gotten up in his face, hooting and hollering, and he possibly pushed, shoved, or slapped her in his defense. I didn't think he would've done anything crazy or beat her up badly. I planned to do more couple's counseling than anything. I could see it being a misunderstanding, mainly because of Princess. She was my cousin, but not by blood. Her mom and my mom have been good friends since high school. Princess was burnt. She had been smoking crack for years and had gone crazy. She wasn't easy on the eyes and was very promiscuous growing up. At this point in her life, she was considered a base-head and no one fucked with her or took her serious.

When I got to Erica's house, Mike was sitting on the couch with a beer in his hand, and a look of despair on his face. When I walked in he popped up and said, "What's up nigga? Whachu want?" I thought to myself, "This nigga is loaded." I asked him where Erica was and he said "Why?" I walked towards her room and Mike got up and tried to stop me. I could've easily kicked Mike's ass and he knew that. The fact that he was intoxicated would've made it even easier. I knew it had to be the liquor that made him think it was a good idea to buck up on me. I walked passed him to see what was wrong with Erica and was shocked. Mike had really done a number on her. She had a black eye, busted lip, and her nose was bleeding. I couldn't think of anything she could've done to make Mike do her like this. I admit, I kind of lost it and started kicking Mike's ass. My goal was to make him look worse than Erica but she stopped me. After the whooping, I couldn't get Mike to leave, so I took Erica and her son to my house for the night.

Mike came by my house the next morning not having much recollection of what happened the night before. He was just bruised up and knew he had fucked up. He wasn't mad at me because he knew he was out of line, but mainly because there was nothing he could do about it. Mike and Erica went outside to talk. Alicia kept her eye on them. They made up and left together.

My hustle continued to slip because I was drunk all of the time. I've been locked up a few times for drunk driving, possession, and not going to court. I was able to bail out on most of the charges because I had a little bit of money saved up. However, I didn't have money for adequate defense. So, I still had to hustle while I was out on bail. I started slanging crack again but I didn't have the same clientele as before and I ended up sitting on it longer than I needed. I knew that I had to do either one of two things: stop drinking or get a job. I tried working but I just wasn't up for it. I wasn't the working type. I was too easy-going and laid back to be busting my ass for some company. Fuck that! Unless, I was in a management position, I wasn't fuckin with it. I had a few weed connects that wanted to put me on but my money was funny and I couldn't take advantage of what they were trying to put me on to. Mike had a patna who slung ecstasy pills in bulk. He wanted me to hook up with him and rob him. So, I told him to set it up. I told Mike that I didn't want to meet his friend, know who he was, or be of any acquaintance. I said, "Just tell the boy you got someone who wants to buy a bunch of pills and to come meet you. Tell me where and I'll be there."

    Mike's boy showed up at an undisclosed spot with about 20,000 pills. When Mike went to meet him, Boog and I hopped out of my car and flashed our burners. He was a mixed kid from the north end of town. He had no business coming to the spot Mike called him to. He must've wanted to get robbed? He was scared shitless! This wasn't our first robbery together. We didn't wear any masks or disguises because we always wanted the person to see the look on our faces. This usually let them know that we meant business. We took all of the pills he had on him and about $5,000 in cash. It was easy pickings! We decided to meet up at my brother's trap spot after the robbery because it was close to where we pulled the lick. Our deal was for Boog and I to split 15,000 pills and Mike would get 5,000 pills. We didn't let him know anything about the money. Mike had an issue with the split and he started to trip with Boog. Boog thought we should've given him less because we did all of the work, but I already bargained for Mike to receive that amount because he set up the robbery. Boog and Mike started to argue over it until Tyree quieted them down. I was imagining how good of a fight it would've been between the two of them. Neither one of them could fight very well. Boog was a little bit bigger than Mike, but Mike may have been quicker. The end result would have been Boog pulling out his gun before it was done and over with. Mike knew it wasn't worth it.

We had pills for sale! This was a good time to have them because ecstasy was the newest thing in the hood and everyone was trying them. They usually went for $15-20 a pop. But we gave stupid deals since we had so many of them. Other people who had them for sale were upset because we flooded the streets. So, we gave them a better deal than what they were getting from their suppliers. We started popping a lot of pills, ourselves. We were high for months!

Mike and Erica had gone through it again. A month after Erica forgave Mike for beating her up, he convinced her to marry him. Her dumb ass went along with it and they eloped at some run-down shack and got a quick sham of a marriage. But this didn't make their problems go away. Mike was still Mike. I stayed out of it unless he put his hands on her. Whenever he did, she would call me and I'd come over only to find that he had split before I showed up. He'd call me later pleading his case but by then I didn't care anymore.

Shit hit the fan about two months into their marriage. Apparently, Princess was telling the truth. Mike was fucking around with her and she had proof with pictures and other people that saw them together. When Erica told me about it, I laughed. I mean, Erica wasn't bad looking. She could be cute if she was a little slimmer and did something with her hair every once in a while. But she was a prom queen compared to Princess! She cried over it on my shoulder one night at the bar. The shit was funny to me. I honestly didn't know what she saw in Mike. Erica was like my little sister. I had to tell her like it was. I said, "Look, you married the muthafucka while the rumor was still lurking. So you were aware of the probability of it being true." I told her that the best advice that I had for her, was for her to go and get tested. I knew my cousin, Princess, was a nasty broad. She promised that she would get tested. But she said that her and Mike hadn't been fucking much anyway. She also said that he might've been smoking something other than weed. She told me that she found a pipe in one of his pockets while doing the laundry about a week prior. I said, "It might've been a weed pipe." She said, "I thought so, too. But the problem is that it didn't smell like weed. We never smoke weed out of pipes. I keep rolling papers handy just in case I have no Swishers. So it wasn't weed." This made me recollect what my brother said about him smoking crack in the past. I told her to leave his ass alone and get her marriage annulled.

    I had a few court appearances for the beefs that I caught a couple of months earlier. I was able to take a deal on the DWI charge. They agreed to give me credit for time served, but I had to get a drug and alcohol evaluation, and possibly some rehab. My possession case was still pending. I got caught with my dope individually wrapped and the bud was bagged up. So the charge was upped to "attempt to distribute". It carried a four-year sentence if I blew trial. I didn't think that they could prove that I was attempting to distribute. I tried to tell them that I bought it like that and that it was for my personal use, but the prosecution wasn't buy it. They told me the only way I could get it lessened to a "simple possession" and avoid jail time was if I told them where and who I got it from. That was out of the question. My public defender said that he could get me 18 months if I pleaded to "possession" but he thought that I had action at trial. We pushed and postponed it for a while.

On the streets, I was still dealing with the antics of this Mike character. It came out that this guy really was smoking crack. Erica told me that he tried to get back with her but she wasn't going for it. She told him that she talked to me and that I advised her to get checked for an STD. Mike looked at this as me siding with Erica in the matter and took it as a sign of disrespect. His way of getting back at me for this was by calling Alicia and telling her about some of the females that I'd been fucking around with. By this time, Mike burned so many bridges around town, people knew better than to believe him. He told a few homies that I was smoking crack with him and was even trying to spread gay rumors. No one believed him. As a matter of fact, a couple of my homies kicked his ass for lying and trying to spread rumors about a real nigga. I didn't trip. I just knew that whenever I found this guy, I was going to beat the shit out of him. I didn't need a weapon because I had no intentions of killing him. But I was going to give him a whippin he wouldn't be able to walk away from.

I was in the South End picking up my homeboy Resins from his girl's house. I knew I was out of bounds but my guy didn't have a solid ride back to the CD. When I pulled up, Resins and his girl were outside talking to Mike. It looked like he was pleading his case to them but Resins wasn't hearing it. He didn't want to hear what this dude had to say or entertain anymore of the rumors that he was spreading. When Mike saw my car he bolted up the block! I started to get out and give chase but he already had a good head start. Resins and his girl hopped into the car and we gave chase. Mike made moves on me. He cut through some houses and lost me a few times. When I finally caught up with him, he was in some white folk's front yard talking on their house phone. When the people saw me pull up, they ducked off into the house. I didn't wanna believe this guy was on the phone calling the cops on me! I said, "Mike, I know you're not calling the cops on me?!" He said, "Yup, and I told them that you have a gun." I thought to myself, "Unbelievable!" For one, he ran from me after talking all of that shit in the streets. Two, he ran into some people's yard and called the cops on me. And three, he told them I was packing! I told him, "Alright dude. That's how you wanna play this out?" Then, I left. The truth is that I didn't have a gun on me at that time. But my license was suspended and I had weed and dope in the car. Resins had a license but they would've searched the car regardless, because of the gun accusation and my criminal history. Resins hopped into the driver's seat and we boned out!

After my last run-in with Mike, I made it my job to let people all around town know what Mike had done. I even went to the South End to let some people out there know. Mike claimed to be from Horton Street. It was in the South End but I knew a lot of them dudes from Horton and I didn't have any existing issues with any of them. I grew up with a couple of them from my Holly Park days and went to Franklin High School with a few of them, too. I went to the corner store where most of them usually hung out. I was with Resins and Boog at the time. Resins didn't have any problem coming with me but Boog had a long running beef with a few of them cats. I planned to get out, converse, and let these dudes know what this guy from their hood had been up to. Boog stayed in the car with his burner cocked off safety. Mike had a few loyal boys in his hood but the dudes from Horton were real. They heard about what

Mike was doing and respected me for coming to their hood to tell them in person. Reggie was a cat that I also knew from the Holly Park days. He was a couple of years older than me and was much bigger. Reggie pretty much ran that hood. Him and I did some jail-time together and had respect for one another. I told him about my issue with Mike, and Reggie said, "You don't have to do anything. We'll take care of it." I don't know what he meant by that but I had to stand my own ground. I said, "Look, Big Homie, with all due respect…I came here to let ya'll know I had an issue with a dude from your hood out of respect. I didn't come here to ask for permission to handle my business. I'm not gonna kill the nigga. But I *am* gonna beat the fuck out of him."

About two weeks had gone by since my last Mike encounter. I told a bunch of people who knew Mike, to call me if they ran into him over the last few weeks. By now, I had grown tired of looking for him. I tried setting him up by having Erica call and set up a meeting to try and reconcile, but that didn't work either. The main reason why I stopped looking for him was because I knew that at the end of the day, all he was going to do was run or call the police. Nobody fucked with snitches in the hood. Plus, I had to face reality myself: he was a crack-head and chasing him around made me look like a crack-head, too.

I was still coming to the hood every day to hustle and had been kicking it with Boog more. Boog started popping pills more regularly. He'd take some ecstasy in the middle of the day, be up all throughout the night, and sleep a good portion of the next day away. He became a vampire. We'd kick it tough on the weekends or days when I stayed in the hood later than usual, to hustle. Boog hustled too. But his pill popping and constantly staying in beefs affected his hustle, severely. When he got thizzed out, he'd become extra "mannish" and would try to flex on cats. He wasn't much of a fighter but if things got hectic he was quick to pull out his pistol. This was cool whenever we would come across sticky situations but not all of them required a gun to be added to the equation. There were times when we were in a club and weren't able to get a pistol in. Boog would be "shit out of luck" when shit popped off. He would have to fight until he was able to make it back to the car. Usually, he was able to defend himself until I jumped in or someone broke things up. But soon after, he'd be posted up outside strapped, waiting for whomever to come outside afterwards. Boog was my dude! But he was known for taking things too far. I ended up in more than enough unprovoked shootings behind him overreacting, or having to fight off more guys than I needed to, because he wasn't able to help out from the shoulders.

Things were going alright with Alicia and I for the time being. I paid for her to complete a nursing assistant course she started a while back. She said that she wanted to get certified so that she could get back into the workforce. She needed to do something besides sit at home with the baby. I didn't know what it was at the time, but she was suffering from post-partum depression and isolated herself. She continued to lash out at me because of me and my doings. But I knew that she had to have known that I wasn't the problem. I admit that I had my part in causing problems in our relationship. I'd be out all day and night and sometimes wouldn't even make it home. When I did come home, I would be drunk, high, and passed out before we were able to spend any quality time together, as a family. At the same time, I tried my best to make things function. I wanted us to work and I had no intentions of giving up at that time. This was my family.

Alicia went to school in the morning and I was left at home with Lil Ty for a good portion of the day. This meant that I couldn't drink as much or do too much driving. My license had been suspended for years and I always had warrants due to my failure to go to court. Whenever I got pulled over it was a wrap. Either, I was going to jail or I was going to engage in a high-speed chase. There were times when I would hop out of the car and take them on a foot chase, but I didn't have the wind for that anymore. I'd been smoking cigarettes for a while and was definitely out of shape. I knew this couldn't go down if I had the baby with me. So, I would usually chill or have a chick pick me up. It was usually a chick that I was messing with on the side that Alicia knew nothing about. I tried my best to keep things cool at home. I knew that I was a piece of shit but I wouldn't admit to being that. I had morals and principles that I stuck to and some that I blatantly disregarded. I made sure that my family was taken care of and all of the bills were paid. But it came to a point where that was all that I could do because of my increasing alcohol addiction. I was a drunk. I would have called myself an alcoholic, but that term is for those who knowingly admit to their addiction. I felt like I could stop whenever I wanted to and I considered myself as a "social drinker" even though I usually drank alone.

It was one of those cool summer days. I spent all day kicking it with Alicia and the baby. We went to my mom's house and chilled for a little, hung out in the hood, and later, we went to the park. It was one of those days when I didn't really care if my phone rang. Erica had been doing some bank licks so I had a couple of extra bucks in my pocket. When we headed home, my youngest brother, CJ, came with us. He was about six years old at the time and wanted to come to my house and play with his little nephew. We decided to grab one of Alicia's little cousins, Jimmy, and Erica's son, Denny, to come hang out, too. Before we got to the house, we grabbed some pizzas and a couple of movies for them to watch. Lil Ty was having a ball! He enjoyed it when other people came over because it was usually just he and his mom at the house alone.

    I had been drinking all day. So, at some point I went back into my room and laid it down. I hadn't quite passed out yet when my phone started ringing. I didn't answer it the first time because I thought it was a joog calling. After it rang two or three more times, I looked and saw it was Boog calling me. I answered and he said, "What's up my nig? I'm in the hood by the am/pm and Mike is over here. You want me to chill and smoke a blunt with him to give you some time to get here?" It was 1 o'clock in the morning. I was drunk, half asleep, and in no position to get up out of my bed, and drive across town to chase Mike's dumb ass around the hood. I told Boog, "Naw, man I ain't coming over there to fuck with that dummy." He said, "Alright. Well, I'm gonna beat him up myself." I said, "Do what you do, homie." I thought to myself about how the situation might play out. Boog was in the hood on some vampire shit trying to catch Mike and beat him up. It didn't seem right. Rather than pondering on it, I decided to go back to sleep.

    Boog called back 10 minutes later and said, "Man, this nigga know what's up, T. He keeps running away from me saying he knows TLEE sent you here." I told Boog to, "Leave that cluck alone and quit wasting your time. You know the boy is a snitch. Whatever you do to him, he's gonna fuck around and tell the cops, and that shit is gonna come back on me. Leave his ass alone!" He said, "Alright", and hung up.

The next morning when I woke up, I immediately went to the fridge to grab a beer. This was usually how I started my mornings to prevent any hangovers. I probably wouldn't know what a hangover looked like. After about an hour, Alicia woke the boys up and started making breakfast. Erica came by to pick up Denny. She came in and looked at me with a blank stare on her face, like she was waiting for me to tell her something. I said, "What's up?" She said, "Don't look at me like you don't know." Confusingly, I replied, "Don't know what?" She could tell that I was puzzled by whatever it was she was implying. She said, "So you don't know?" By now, I was kind of frustrated and said, "NO...WHAT?!" She said, "Mike got shot last night." I thought to myself, "Aww, fuck..." I asked Erica "Is he alright?" You see, I wasn't trying to kill the boy. I just wanted to kick his ass real good. Mike and I were friends at one point. I knew Mike's mom and brother. They all knew he was a piece of shit and understood my frustrations with him. I even told them I was going to kick his ass when I ran into them. They just told me not to beat him up too bad.

After processing what Erica told me, I started having vivid recollections of the phone conversation that Boog and I had from the night before, and then I put one and two together. I asked her, "Where did he get shot at?" She said, "In his ass", which caused me to laugh for a quick second at the thought of it, but then I quickly realized how this could potentially affect me. Mike probably thought I told Boog to shoot him and might've told the police some dumb shit like that. After I thought more about it, I called Boog but he didn't answer. I called a couple more times with no success. Later, I went by his house and his roommate, Cliff, said that he hadn't seen Boog since the day before. I was gonna go visit and see Mike in the hospital but I didn't like how the scenario played out in my head. There might have been cops there, or his family might trip and think I had something to do with him being shot. So, I didn't go. Later in the day, Erica called me after she went to visit Mike in the hospital. She said that he was saying that Boog shot him, but claimed that I was there too. She didn't believe him because Alicia already told her that I was at home all night.

    Erica and I had been working on a few accounts with my aunt. She had a couple of profiles that were manageable for Erica to work. Erica, my aunt, one of my aunt's friends named Jenna, and I had been out trying to cash as many checks as we could before the banks caught on. Jenna was this crazy White girl my aunt had known for years. She was crazy cool, had a valid driver's license, and was a hell of a driver. She knew where all the good banks to hit were located. We actually had fun working! We would go way out north and then head east. Erica rarely had issues getting the checks cashed because she was light-skinned to the point that she almost looked white. She always stayed calm, cool, and collect. Auntie's paperwork was always on point. Erica was also good at recognizing the warning signs and always managed to get out with all of the paperwork before the authorities were alerted. You'd rarely find teamwork like this! Afterwards, we'd go back to my aunt's house and split the money. We'd roll a couple of blunts, have drinks, and make plans for the next day.

Erica and I became tighter because of the whole Mike ordeal. I was really just trying to put some money in both of our pockets. But my main objective was to coach her into telling me the lowdown on Mike. She had grown away from him since the ordeal but I talked her into creating a line of communication between them to see where his head was. She said that he wasn't planning anything but she realized that he was falling deeper into his addiction. I thought of that as a good thing. It meant that he wasn't talking to the police about Boog and I. Erica and I would meet up and hang out at the local bar and talk about a potential strategy to confront him with, so he wouldn't tell. I assured her that we weren't gonna kill him. Erica wasn't in love with him anymore but she didn't want to see him get hurt any more than he already had. Erica was a crooked bitch herself but like most females she had a conscience. She knew that if we killed Mike, it would fuck with her for the rest of her life. I knew I had to gain her trust.

It had been a couple of weeks since I last talked to Boog. He still wasn't answering my phone calls. One day, I thought, "fuck it", and popped up at his house for a surprise visit. Cliff answered the door without asking who it was first. I looked in and saw Boog and went after his ass! He tried to run but I grabbed him and threw him to the ground. He yelled, "T, whachu doing?!" I said, "Nigga, why the fuck you been ducking me?!" We tussled for a minute until he swung at me in self-defense, then I dropped him with a left to the jaw! It didn't knock him out but it made him realize who he was fucking with! I helped him get back up and got his attention. I confronted him about this whole Mike thing and told him how dumb it was for him to shoot his dumb ass. I told him how it had the potential to backfire on us, both. I asked the simple question, "Why?" Boog looked me dead in my eyes and said, "Because he ran." I shook my head in disagreement with his stupidity. I told him that this shit was all him. I assured him that if the cops came and asked me anything about the situation, that I wouldn't mention his name and play dumb-fuck. He assured me that this was his beef and he wouldn't let me get tangled up in it. He said he'd take care of it. I never asked him how he planned to take care of it. I just trusted that he would take care of it.

The following weeks were kind of hazy. I found myself kicking it with Erica more often. I'd always be in the CD hustling and would end up at her house while running around. Or I'd stop by her house to go over some information regarding hitting some bank licks. I wasn't sexually attracted to Erica; or at least I didn't feel that way towards her. I knew she more than likely had feelings for me, but she knew that I was out of bounds because of her close relationship with Alicia. Erica was known for being easy and I knew that she had been with her fair share of guys. For that reason, I knew that I wouldn't hit it. Also, fucking her would be playing too close to home. I mean...I've messed around with girls who were good friends before; but not when one of them was my child's mother and live-in girlfriend. We kept things really casual. My thoughts were of her looking at me like a big brother.

Auntie had some accounts for us to hit but she had a small problem. Our driver, Jenny, was arrested a few days earlier on some outstanding warrants. She was our only driver and we really didn't fuck with anyone else. Another problem was that my aunt wasn't going to be able to go with us because she had to tend to Grandma and take her to a few doctor's appointments. She had three checks that had to be cashed *today* and couldn't wait until tomorrow. Erica and I didn't have a valid driver's license, nor did we have time to look for someone who did. We decided that if we were going to do this and drive my car, we had to go right now. We said, "fuck it", and went.

    Things were going good. The first two went off with no problem. She used two different identities and came out of both banks with cash. We figured that the last one would be a cinch. She went inside the bank, calm and collect as usual. She was usually in the bank for about 4-5 minutes unless there were long lines. I knew that if she took more than 10 minutes, something could be wrong. She had been in this bank for 15 minutes and I was sweating bullets! I just knew that she was being stalled for the cops! I was parked across the street at the gas station so that I could see her come out. We had signals to alert each other when something went wrong. Erica wore glasses. But when she went into the bank she would wear a hat or something on her head. If she came out of the bank and just took her glasses off, things were cool. I'd leave from my post and pick her up from the nearest corner. If she came out of the bank and just took off her hat or headpiece, and walked in the opposite direction in which she came in, that meant that there was a problem and to meet her out of sight. Our most important signal was if she came out of the bank and took both her glasses and hat off, it meant that things were all bad, and the police were more than likely called. This signal called for me to pick her up wherever, quickly leave the area, and dispose of any other information that was in the vehicle. This happened on more than one occasion. Getting rid of the paperwork was crucial in these circumstances, in case the cops stopped us. One time, we had to split and still had a bunch of checks in the car. Jenny was on the freeway going way over the speed limit, while Erica, my aunt, and I disposed of the evidence. We were ripping shit into shreds and trying to throw it out of the window without being seen by other drivers. Aunt Vernice's method was to rip the checks down as small as possible, then she would eat the paper. This was how we got rid of shit in extreme circumstances. But today, Erica came out of the bank and just took off her glasses. Apparently, her teller had a computer issue that took a minute to resolve.

    It was later in the day when we met up with my aunt. She was at Grandma's house waiting on us. We put a portion of each of our cuts towards bailing Jenny out. We knew we couldn't have any more close calls without her there. We had a couple of drinks with my aunt and then Erica and I left. The Mike issue came up again and the conversation led to what to say if the police got involved and decided to question us? So, instead of me dropping her off at her car, we went to a nearby bar to further discuss the issue. We were there for about an hour going over our story before the alcohol started kicking in. Another couple came up to us in the bar and started a conversation with us. We ended up playing darts and shooting pool with them. We were kind of drunk, having a good time conversing. They must've thought that Erica and I were a couple because they were asking us question like, "How long have ya'll been together?" and "How many kids do you have?" We were really loaded by then so we just played it off and continued playing. When we left, I planned to take Erica back to her car but she said, "Just take me home. I'm too drunk to drive. I'll come get my car tomorrow." I was loaded myself. I don't know how I made it to her house without getting pulled over.

When we got to her house, I decided to walk in with her and drink some water to try and sober up a little bit before driving home. I ended up passing out on her couch. I woke up about an hour later and Erica was laying on me. I didn't think anything of it at first because I figured that she was just as loaded as I was. So, I let her lay on me. Her hands started wandering and my body reacted much differently than what my mind was telling me. She started rubbing her hands up and down my chest and it was kind of soothing, but I knew it was wrong. She went a little too far and touched the pipe; which was harder than granite. She put her hand down my pants and stroked it a few times. I said, "Erica, what are you doing?" She started kissing me on my chest as she moved towards my dick and said, "I don't know?" She put my dick in her mouth and started blowing me. I wanted to tell her to stop but I couldn't. I thought to myself, "This is so wrong!" It was by far one of the best blowjobs that I had ever had! She was sucking my dick like she meant to! It would've been a violation of all penis treaties if I made her stop. All I could think about was "What would happen if Alicia found out?" After she sucked my dick for about 5 minutes, things got even more heated when we made our way to her bedroom. I was as wrong as two left shoes! But I was drunk and caught in the moment. I didn't understand what I was doing or why she decided to take it there but I was with it for the time being. We got to the bedroom and had incredible sex! That fact that we both knew it was wrong was the reason why we got such a thrill out of it. Maybe this was the only way she felt like she could repay me for helping free her of Mike and putting her on with my aunt to make some extra money? I still to this day don't know the answer to that. But if this was her way of saying thanks, I forgot to say, "You're welcome".

    The next day, we got up and headed back to my aunt's house. I tried my best to act like nothing happened the night before. So, I just focused on the job at hand. Auntie had two checks that needed to be cashed before this particular account dried out. The checks were for about $4,000 each. So, we had to be very cautious of our surroundings. Auntie told Erica not to let them stall her like last time because we obviously couldn't afford it. She agreed and we left. We decided to hit up the east side. After she went in to cash the second check at the second bank, my aunt and I started talking about our next venture. We talked about the possibilities of adding more people to the scheme but she was reluctant to whom. Auntie was very picky about who she did business with. She had been doing this for a minute and had been caught up before. She did some time behind cashing bad checks but learned how to perfect it and reduce her chances of being caught. She liked Erica but had reservations because of her dealings with Mike. Also, she wasn't sure how she would act under pressure. I assured her that Mike was out of the picture and that I felt like she was truer to the game than she came off to be. She threw me for a loop when she said, "You know that girl is in love with you?" I said, "What?" She said, "Trust me nephew. I see how she looks at you, talks about you, and how she's always willing to do anything for you." I replied, "Naw, Auntie. She's just loyal and she respects a real nigga." Auntie said, "You can feed that bullshit to whoever you want but I know it's more than that!" I remained quiet. If it was visible to her that something was going on, who else could notice? After Erica came out of the last bank, we headed back to house, divided up the cash, and went our separate ways.

I went home after leaving my aunt's house because I hadn't seen Alicia and Lil Ty in three days. She was upset when I got home. She went off, called me a bunch of names, saying how I was probably up to no good, and accused me of being laid up with some other bitch, etc. I told her what I had been doing and that I crashed at my mom's house the night before because I was too drunk to drive home. She didn't buy it but couldn't think of anything to come back with. I stayed home for the next two days and kissed her ass to get back on her good side. It always took a couple of days to get back on good terms with her.

A lot happened over the next couple of months. Erica got arrested twice after trying to cash a couple of checks. She spent a couple of days in jail each time and didn't say anything to the cops. The first time, she was released on her own recognizance. She didn't have a criminal history so bail wasn't necessary. We had to bail her out on the second charge. The charges stayed pending but she wasn't looking at any hard time. We had sex twice more during this time, but I stopped because I felt like she was getting too attached. I knew this was gonna backfire on me in some way, so I felt like I had to stop before she fell in too deep. I don't think she wanted to be with me in particular. But she wanted a nigga like me. No one knew that we were messing around except us. We acted normal when we were around other people but she got mushy whenever we were alone.

My cousin Jay was released after spending three years in the joint. Jay and I were still tight and kept in contact while he was down. People said we looked alike. We looked even more alike when we had similar hairstyles. I was taller, but Jay was bigger. I introduced him to Erica. Not to hook them up, but just as an introduction. I could say it was love at first sight, but it was always that way with Jay. He wore his heart on his sleeve just like his dad, my Uncle Jerome. They both fell hard for pretty or moderately cute women. Jay saw how Erica was making money, and she was fairly good looking, so he eventually made a play at her. Jay wasn't the smartest guy in the family and was known for making dumb decisions without giving a fuck. But he was one of the more charismatic ones of the bunch. It was obvious that Jay took a liking to her and the attraction was mutual. Of course, I didn't mind it. It was a way that I could get Erica's mind off of me. I was planning to tell Jay that I had been with her before but he was also known for being a blabbermouth. I mean…he could've already expected that I had hit it, just by knowing how I got down. But I didn't tell him outright. I wasn't going to say anything if he didn't ask. Their little relationship blossomed from day one and I went back to doing what I did best. Hustling!

"You can act as hard as you want to but we all know the truth about who we really are. We let our ego do the talking for the most part but our thoughts of being inadequate raises doubt in the belief we have in ourselves. We are our own biggest critics and we are constantly putting ourselves in situations that our character isn't capable of keeping us."

Tough Talk

2003 - 2005

It was nearing the holiday season when my mom called me with some startling news. She said that I got a letter in the mail from the King County prosecutor. It said that I was being charged with first degree assault. My first thought was that it had to have been a mistake. I heard that Mike was talking to the cops but I didn't think anything could stick with me. I figured that Boog was going to be cooked no matter what, but to add me to the equation was going to make any case complicated because I had a legitimate alibi. When I showed up to court, I found out that Mike lied and said that I was there with Boog when he got shot. Erica said that he tried to concoct that story when he was in the hospital but I didn't think anything would become of it. I read his official statement and it said that I was there shooting with Boog. I thought to myself, "Who would even believe this guy and this bullshit story?" They planned to hold me on $100,000 bail! I told the prosecutor that my lawyer was in the hallway and asked if it was alright if I went and grabbed him? I went out into the hallway and made a break for it!

After leaving the courtroom, I made a couple of moves to prepare myself for what was laying ahead. First, I contacted Boog. He was already aware of the charges and had no intentions of turning himself in. Boog intended to stay in the streets as long as he could and not worry about the case until he got picked up. I thought about going back to Jamaica but I had too much to lose in doing that. I had a son, a girl, and things were much more serious this time. I would've been in Jamaica for a lot longer than I was the last time and they might've even came to get me, and press additional charges.

I contacted a lawyer, Jim Roe, which my Uncle Jerome referred to me. He advised me to come down and have a talk with him and to bring $1,000. I met up with the lawyer and told him everything that I knew. He was my lawyer so I knew that he was bound by privilege not to reveal anything that I told him. He said he was going to set up a new court date and plead with the judge to grant a conditional release while we pieced together our case. He also said that he would try to get it thrown out due to lack of evidence. The judge ruled that I be detained but reduced my bail to $50,000, which was $5,000 bondable. I spent three days in jail before my mom and aunt came to bail me out. This put a serious dent in my pockets but I don't think that I could have adequately fought this case while in custody.

I had a couple of options. My first option was to fight this case. My only problem was that my co-defendant was Boog and he was guilty as sin. He even got caught with the gun that he shot Mike with a month after the incident. He only spent a week or two in jail before being released. This was complicated to me and I didn't know how he got out of that circumstance or how my name got thrown into this case. My second option was to apprise my lawyer of everything I knew. But I quickly disagreed and disregarded it as an option. My lawyer told me that I could sever the case and testify against Boog. He said if I did this, the most I would get was 3-6 months in jail and probation. I wasn't a snitch nor would I ever let myself be classified as one! I told him that wasn't an option either. My third option was simple: kill Mike Huntley. It seemed simple enough until I spoke with some of my older homies and they told me about the negative consequences from going that route. I spoke with my big homie Butchie about that option and he convincingly said, "Yeah T, that's a viable option. But other issues may arise and you might have to kill more people to cover up any other issues or tie up loose ends. If you kill the boy, you're gonna have to kill the bitch too." He meant Erica.

Butchie said that he spoke with my dad and that my dad told him to advise me to find a plea deal. The only problem with that was that there wasn't a reasonable plea on the table. They offered me 6 years. There was no way I was going to plea to that shit! However, if I blew trial I would be looking at 25 years! I still couldn't plead guilty to a crime that I didn't commit!

About a month later, Boog got picked up. He was hiding out at his mom's house when they came and got him. He called me after he was booked and tried to tell me how to play the case. I told him he had to be crazy to think I was going to listen to anything he had to say! I'd been trying to talk to him for weeks about it and he just avoided me! I remember him saying, "as long as we stuck to our story we would be cool". I knew that wouldn't work because he had no story, no alibi, and the people who were going to testify and say that I wasn't there when the shooting occurred, couldn't say the same for him. I agreed with him because I felt like I had to at that point. He was in custody and could eventually start singing false tunes that the prosecutor might be able to use as leverage.

This case was taking its toll on me and I was constantly worried about doing hard time. There were times when I felt like the walls were closing in on me, and sometimes I felt like I had no one in my corner to help me, but I tried to stay focused. I was still hustling but my excessive drinking limited my ability to make money. At this point, I wasn't hustling to pay the rent for the apartment that Alicia, Lil Ty, and I were living in. I was hustling to pay my lawyer fees. My intentions were to fight this case!

I was walking up Cherry Street when the gang unit police picked me up. Apparently, they've been watching me for a while and decided to pick me up on a warrant. I was drunk when they arrested me and took me back to the police station. Jack Javorski was the lead detective on the case. I knew his intentions were to talk to me about the Mike Huntley shooting but he was trying to be slick about it. He started talking to me about my dad, my uncles, and my cousin Jay. As soon as he started to mention Boog and Mike's name, I immediately asked for my lawyer. Dt. Lundbar came shortly after that. I didn't know what to think. This guy had been on my case for years! He walked in and didn't say anything. He just listened as Dt. Javorski laid out the details on my recent whereabouts and how fucked I was. I didn't respond. I was waiting on my lawyer.

When my lawyer arrived he was heated! He yelled at both of the detectives for continuing to communicate with me after I already requested my attorney. They tried to book me on my warrants but my lawyer got me released because they picked me up under false pretenses.

I started meeting with my lawyer more often to discuss our approach to my case. I still couldn't understand how this lying muthafucka got the police and the prosecutor to believe his bullshit story! This shit was affecting multiple areas of my life and causing a great amount of stress. The prosecutor kept offering me deals that a guilty man wouldn't even agree to! The first deal entailed a seven-year plea agreement if I pled to first-degree assault. It was nuts that my attorney would even mention that offer! But ethically, he had to inform me of all of the deals offered by the prosecutor. They offered another deal for 5 years, but I turned it down as well. I got a letter from the prosecutor's office that said they were amending the charges to attempted murder. This charge carried a possible 30-year sentence if I was found guilty of all charges. There was also a gun enhancement charge added because there was a gun involved.

I was still hustling to make ends meet. I found myself drinking more, smoking more weed, and even popping pills to null the worries that I had going on in my head. The increase in my drug habit, along with the worry from the case, caused Alicia and I to argue and fight more. She had my back but she would constantly talk about what I wasn't doing for her. I found her to be obtuse in her angles of approaches towards me in my psychological state. It caused me to be out in the streets more. I was exhibiting negative behaviors that were counter-productive to what was going on in my life. I was still paying all of the bills because she wasn't working. I paid for her to go to school to get her nursing assistant certificate and even paid for her to get her license to practice in the field, but she still didn't attempt to get a job. This could've helped me out significantly! Whenever I would bring up the topic of her working so I could focus more on paying for my defense, she complained about childcare. She knew that we had numerous family members who would have no problem watching Lil Ty while she worked. I figured that she was being lazy, inconsiderate, and selfish. Most of our arguments took place while I was intoxicated. Sometimes things got physical. I used to tell myself and everyone else that everything was her fault, because I believed that. It was her fault that I was paying all of the bills because she wouldn't work. It was her fault that I had a drug habit because I had to fuel myself with something before coming home to hear her bullshit. It was her fault that I was in this legal predicament because Erica and Mike were her friends. If I weren't with her, I wouldn't be in the position that I was in. I even blamed her for me putting hands on her when I did. Alicia was a fighter. When things got physical, it was usually her throwing the first couple of blows before I would retaliate. But I was a man and should've never put my hands on her no matter the case. When I added everything up and was able to evaluate myself, I still believed that she was the problem. But I was wrong for still being with her. I knew we weren't meant for each other and especially at that time. As the case got deeper, my stress built up. It led to me not going home at all and staying wherever I had my last drink at. Often times, I would wake up in unfamiliar places, not knowing how I got there. Alicia wouldn't call until after the second day of me being gone. We'd argue some more and it would take me another couple of days to go home. I would stop by to visit with Lil Ty for a of couple hours in between times, but I would avoid her as much as possible.

One day, I got a call from Aunt Vernice that sent me tripping! She asked me if I heard anything about a murder that took place at the bowling alley a couple of days earlier. I told her that I heard about it but I didn't know any of the particulars or what actually happened. She said, "Well, our peoples are locked up for it." I asked her who and she replied, "The Jerome's." Apparently, my cousin Jay and his dad, my Uncle Jerome, had been booked for a murder. What was crazy about it was that the guy they were accused of killing was one of Jay's closest patnas! I didn't understand. I just knew that they were probably gonna end up spending the rest of their lives in prison. It was all bad for us Lee's. There was going to be another generation of us in prison.

The guy that my cousin Jay and my Uncle Jerome were accused of killing was a guy named Chris. His family was heated about the situation and intended to retaliate. The only place that they knew about any of us being at was where my grandma lived. So, we figured that this was where they were gonna try to hit first. Tyree, a couple of homeboys, and I did some quick, strategic planning for when they came. We had to send a message.

The niggas came the next day around dusk. When they pulled up to my grandma's house, we were waiting and already in position. Grandma's house was on top of a hill and you could see people coming from about six to seven blocks way. We already sent Grandma to Auntie Vernice's house the night before. It was me, Tyree, Dank, about 10 more of our patnas, waiting for them. They came two cars deep but that wasn't enough. As soon as we recognized who they were we opened fire! They started to retreat but we gave chase with double the amount of cars they sent. Our young homie, JP, was driving one of the cars. JP's brother, Drake, was riding with him and they were down for whatever! They got into a high-speed chase on the freeway with guns blazing! After about two or three miles of chasing these cats at speeds greater than 80 miles per hour, the police got into it. That was our plan. When they got into the mix, Tyree and I veered our cars off of the highway at the next exit. JP and Drake continued to give chase until the assailant's cars got stopped by the police, then they veered off. The police only chased JP and Drake for another mile or two before heading back to the other dude's cars.

Tyree, Dank, and I went to Chris' momma's house. First, we rolled down the block that she lived on and saw that her door was wide open and that there were a couple of people on the porch. We parked around the corner and walked through her backyard and around to the front, so nobody had a chance to run. We spooked the shit out of them! They could obviously see that we were armed. It was Chris' mom, sisters, his older brother, and his cousin Drag. Drag picked up the phone when he saw us, but Dank and Tyree put a stop to that as soon as he started talking. Tyree said:

"Whoever you're calling is either on the freeway dead or being arrested by the police! I want you guys to know that we are the wrong family to come after! What happened to Chris was unfortunate and you guys have our deepest condolences. But I promise you many more funeral arrangements will have to be made, if attempts are made on my grandma's house. This is unacceptable! And we will always retaliate twice as hard as you attack! We came here with intentions to kill ya'll but we're giving you the opportunity to cease this shit! If not, we know where

y'all grandma stays too! We don't wanna kill if we don't have to! Next time there will be no talking!"

We left. Word quickly spread around town about how we spoiled their retaliation. Tyree and I were looked at much differently, but in similar ways. I was respected and Tyree was feared. People feared me because of Tyree. People respected Tyree because…they feared him.

Jay ended up in the same tank as Boog in the county jail. They didn't know each other personally, but they met a few times and knew of each other. Let me tell you something about my cousin Jay. He was loyal but as gullible as they came. Essentially, he was a smart dude but he knowingly made dumb decisions. He befriended people easily and was socially awkward. He was a killer but had a conscience. This made him unpredictable to those who didn't know him. If you had a proper universal greeting towards him, he befriended you. Boog was manipulative to an extent; mainly, as a persuasion tactic and for self-preservation measures. He and Boog connected easily due to their shared legal state and that they were both kin to me.

I was picked up a few more times on warrants but was able to bail out. Even though I had this trial pending, the judge always allowed bail because my lawyer made it clear that the warrants were old and in no way were connected to the current pending case. Every time I got picked up, Javorski or Lundbar would try to start questioning me about the case and I would lawyer up real quick. One time, they picked me up while I was walking out of a bar. I was drunk when they took me to the station and cornered me in the interrogation room. They promised me that if I told them what happened that night that they would have the prosecutor go easy on me. I kept telling them that I wasn't there but they didn't believe me. Lundbar looked at me as a liar because of our prior history. I always lied to him or led him astray. So, even when I was telling the truth, he still didn't believe me. They asked me about Mike and Boog's beef and how it started. I replied that I did not know. I thought about it and asked them, "If you guys know that the beef was between Mike and Boog, then why am I being charged?" They looked at each other as if they were stumped. They were silent for a moment before leaving the room. They came with something for me to sign and I refused. I was tired by this time. I was drunk and ready to go to jail and sleep it off before bailing out. I said, "Come on man. Take me to the bing so I can get booked in. I'm tired." Javorski said, "Here, sign this form. All it says is that you were here tonight talking about the case on your own volition. If you sign it, I'll let you go home." I agreed and they released me from the police station.

I continued to hustle and tried to maintain my shitty lifestyle. My relationship with Alicia wasn't getting any better. I opted out before it got worse. She wasn't going to stop being a disrespectful bitch and I had no immediate plans to stop my drinking, drugging, or thuggin. My money was funny, my legal situation was killing me, and my alcoholism was growing worse. I told her that I was moving out. I knew that there was no way that I could continue to be in a relationship with her and deal with the stress that I was going through in my life. I tried my best to not make it all about me because I knew that's exactly where she was going to point the blame anyway. In reality, it was more about her than anything. I came to the conclusion that she wasn't a rider. I needed someone by my side to help me through this. I know she never thought that she would be with someone in my predicament. But this shit was real. I was looking at a lot of time and all I had on my side was my mom, my brother, and a couple of female friends who actually cared about me. I was grateful to have them. Alicia didn't take things too well and called me every name that she could think of! She even called me a deadbeat dad, although, I was taking care of her and my son. I cared for her but I just couldn't be with her anymore under my alcoholic-stressed mental state. I envisioned myself coming home drunk one day and getting into an altercation with her and hurting her badly. I hated having these types of visions, and I felt like it was best for us to part ways at that time. I knew that we would eventually be back together in the future, but not now. She had to become a statistical baby momma and deal with those stressors in order to realize how good of a dude I could have been, if only, I had the proper support. I had some major issues of my own to deal with before I was going to be any good for anyone else.

 I went and stayed at my mother's house. I was comfortable at my mom's house because it was in the hood and it was easier for me to make money there. Alicia went to stay with her cousin Tamika. Tamika was another unemployed, single Black female, with multiple kids. Alicia had always been close to her but often talked about her situation and how she would never want to end up like her. But after a few weeks of living with her, things definitely began to change. They started hanging out and going to nightclubs together. When I heard from other people about how Alicia was acting, I would always act like I didn't care, but it ate me up inside. Later, I was hearing about her messing around with other dudes; even some dudes that I knew! She was really starting to show her ass around town! I figured that she was doing this just to get back at me. It hurt but I just stayed focused on hustling and trying to find ways to fight my case. By this time, I had two other charges pending that I knew I was going to have to do some time behind. I didn't care. I could do a year or two. Shit, maybe even three or four years, if needed. But there was no way that I was going to do double-digit years for some shit that I didn't even do! I knew that I had gotten away with some heinous crimes in my lifetime. If I was charged in any of those crimes, I would've stood tall in those matters. But I couldn't let this case do me in. I couldn't let Mike have the last laugh.

  I got a call from Jay. He was telling me about some shit Boog was on. Apparently, he got a statement from his lawyer that was provided to him by Detective Javorski. He said that the letter said that I gave Boog up. The letter said that I told them that I wasn't there, didn't have anything to do with the shooting, and that the beef was between Mike and Boog. The cops put something together, put my name on it, and presented it to Boog as my official statement to make it look like I told on him! What was worse was that he was running with it. He was heated and had every right to be, at first glance. Even though a majority of the shit was true, I never actually said these things or signed a statement saying so. I was drunk and put my name down on a piece of paper so that I could go to sleep. I wasn't aware that the police were legally able to use this type of deception to coerce people against one another. All of that shit was misunderstood. I couldn't believe Boog took this shit the way that he did. I heard him in the background saying shit like, "Niggas don't want me to start talking. If I go down, then everybody's going down!" He could've came at me correct and found out that it was bullshit and kept any other beliefs to himself. He knew that I was way more thorough than that. I had multiple opportunities to give him up, but I didn't. We were co-defendants and I made sure it stayed that way. This meant that we couldn't say anything against each other. I could have easily had my case severed and testified against him months ago! The most amount of time I would've gotten was 6 months, plus probation. I'm the one who had everything to lose, but I was riding this shit out! I was the only one who was actually innocent of any wrong doing in this case. I mean, sure, I'm the one who had beef with Mike. But I didn't shoot him, I didn't tell anyone to shoot him, nor was I present when he was shot! Boog didn't take any of this into consideration. He felt like if he was going down, then everyone else was going down with him. He even threatened to tell the cops that he got the gun from my brother. He was saying all of this on the jail phone! That's how mad he was at that point. There was only one thing I couldn't understand…why wasn't my cousin Jay stomping a mud hole in his ass?

Boog's attempts to spread the word that I snitched on him mostly fell on deaf ears. Everyone that knew me and everyone who knew about the case knew the real. Of course there were a few haters who tried to soak it up, but I checked them or either my real patnas or OG's did. The antics of this dude led me to question my judgment in dealing with some of my other homies.

Police authorities were losing a lot of cases and more crimes were going unsolved due to the "no snitching" campaign that the black community started in America. It was hard for them to find witnesses inside and outside of jail. Law enforcement leveled the playing ground by the type of control they had inside of county jails. They began orchestrating something called "Inmate Task Force" (ITF). This was when they would purposely house undercovers or informants in tanks with another inmate they needed information from regarding certain cases. They succeeded in blending them in with the population. Word got back to the prosecutor about my cousin Jay's case because of his gullible ass. He befriended a guy who was in his unit and constantly talked to him about things that had nothing to do with his case. Jay's defense was that he didn't do it. His alibi was Erica and it was shaky. I mean, she was down, but no one knew how she would hold up under pressure. They had evidence of a rocky relationship between Jay and the victim, him being placed at the bowling alley before the murder occurred, and some forensic evidence that could possibly place him at the scene of the crime. Jay felt confident about the case and that he had action at winning because their witness testimony was weak and their evidence was circumstantial.

As Jay became more comfortable with this particular individual who entered his unit, the more he revealed. Ultimately, he ended up telling him the truth. Jay revealed that it was murder, and that he had little to no remorse about the fact that the dude was dead. They had gotten into it over a "drug deal gone bad" multiple times, and Jay was fed up with him. Once the guy reported back to the prosecution with what Jay had told him, they used it as leverage to get a plea out of Jay. He ended up pleading to manslaughter and his dad, who actually didn't do anything, pled to rendering and criminal assisting. Jay got 12 years and Uncle Jerome got three.

I got word from my attorney that Boog was yelling all types of shit from the county jail. It was actually working in my favor because the truth started to come out. The ITF agents relayed back to the prosecutor that Boog, indeed, acted alone. This made it possible for them to drop any gun possession charges against me. And my story about not being at the scene of the crime was becoming more credible. But I still had to fight. The prosecution was now beginning to believe I orchestrated the whole ordeal! By this time, I had to fire my attorney because I couldn't afford him anymore and I was assigned a public defender. It was ironic that I was assigned the same public defender that my brother Tyree was assigned when he shot Paul. I didn't like him because he defended me like he knew that I was guilty. He was looking for a plea bargain from day one. He knew that I didn't want to plea but he also knew that I wasn't going to testify either. My public defender's name was Craig McDonald. He had been a lawyer in Seattle for over 20 years and defended both, adults and juveniles. He was an overweight white man who seemed fearless in the courtroom. Craig was legally blind but it didn't hamper his ability to try a case. I asked my former attorney, Jim Roe, about him and he said, "Craig is a good lawyer. I wouldn't recommend you going to trial with him. But he'll get you a good deal." This would've sounded good for a guilty person but I was the anomaly. I had a couple more run-ins with the law, received more threats from Boog, and my alcoholism was leading to depression.

I was talking with my brother one night and he noticed how things were taking its toll on me, psychologically. We were on some brotherly bonding shit but it was more like a scolding. Tyree decided to tell me about myself and suggested that I started taking responsibility for the mistakes that I've made and try something new. He said, "Ty, you are the coldest hustler that I know and one of the smoothest guys in the hood. You're intelligent, methodical, and observant in all aspects of the game of life, and you have been my teacher from day one. I mostly learn from your successes and mistakes. You've done all this while being a killer. That's why I can't see how you are letting this situation fuck with you like this. I've never known you to have a conscience." He was right. I had grown soft. And I was letting this situation get the best of me. I told Tyree, "I feel you little bro. I'm gonna clean up my act and fight this case." He said, "No, nigga! Just take a plea! I'll deal with Mike and Boog. They won't be able to tie you to anything if you're in jail." I argued with him about it to no avail. He was set on doing what he planned to do. I left it alone and called a meeting with my lawyer.

    I wasn't content about pleading to something that I didn't do. I was talking to my Uncle Tommy about it and he took the "realist" approach regarding the matter. Uncle Tommy said, "Nigga, two – three years for something you didn't do? If you didn't do it, then why are you being charged? You definitely had more than just a minimal role in the matter." I told him about how it felt bad on my conscience to even consider taking a plea and about how Mike straight lied. I told him that I felt like I'd be playing the role of a fool if I went to jail for this shit! Uncle Tommy knew me better than I thought he did. He knew that the real reason why I was so upset was that I hated being outsmarted. Especially, by someone that I knew wasn't smarter than me. Uncle Tommy said, "Ty, look at all the shit you've done that you never got caught for. Then look at all the shit you actually got away with. If you got caught for that shit, would you be doing less than two years?" I said, "No, I'd be underneath the jail." He said, "Exactly! You win some! You lose some! Everybody plays the fool sometimes! Even geniuses! If you ever get a chance, try looking up how many times Einstein failed before coming up with his theory of relativity. He was the town idiot for years before he got his formula right."

    I knew I was going to end up going to jail. But for what and how long was the question? I started to become more reckless out in the streets. My alcoholism affected my hustle, my relationships with women, my family, and my homies. I was involved in a couple of fights that led to me getting arrested and I caught another drug possession charge. My lawyer was trying to broker me a deal doing as little jail time as possible, but he couldn't get anything under two years. That included running my other pending charges concurrent. I didn't have much to work with by now due to the other charges that I had pending. The new charges carried just as much time! I was in the county jail one day waiting to get released on an old warrant that I just posted bail on. I was talking to this cat named Def who was in the same tank. Def was this older dude from Union who beat a murder charge back in the day and once accepted a plea to an attempted murder beef that he claimed he didn't do. He told me about an Alford Plea. I hadn't known anything about it. An Alford Plead was:

> *"A guilty plea of a defendant who proclaims he is innocent of the crime, and admits that the prosecution has enough evidence to prove that he is guilty beyond a reasonable doubt. The defendant*

therefore takes advantage of the prosecutors plea deal without admitting guilt, because of the evidence weighed against them."

Although the evidence was shaky and circumstantial, there was still a good chance that I could be found guilty and do some real time. Especially, fucking with Boog's dumb ass! I talked with my lawyer about an Alford Plea when I got out. He told me that he had to check with the prosecutor and that he might be okay with that since I've been proclaiming my innocence the entire time. My lawyer was still trying to get all of my charges to be run concurrently even though I was looking at 3 years for the possession alone because of my priors.

The prosecutor agreed to accept my plea agreement if I pled to 2nd degree assault. If I pled to 2nd degree assault, he would run all of my other charges concurrently. But he wanted me to allocate to the assault. There must've been a blind spot that he didn't recognize? By agreeing to accept my Alford's Plea, it made the allocation a null notion. He couldn't even use me to testify against Boog if they wanted to try that angle. I attempted to get sympathy from the sentencing judge during my allocution by pleading my innocence as a reason for leniency. My sentencing range was 18-24 months with the plea deal. If I blew trial on all of my charges, I would've gotten 20 years at the minimum. Boog was looking at 30-40 years if he blew trial. The prosecutor wouldn't offer him anything less than 12 years. By me accepting my deal, it made the prosecution's case against Boog weaker and they lost leverage. They couldn't use me as a pawn if they tried.

I was never going to tell on Boog. Even though he was talking reckless, sending threats, and demonstrating numerous acts of disloyalty, I would've never taken the stand. After he started pulling his shenanigans, I started looking for a deal. I actually helped him out by taking a deal because it was an Alford's Plea. They offered him 7 years.

"I believe that the criminal justice system was created under numerous amounts of misunderstandings, as society attempted to punish those who broke historically, unfair laws. I feel that instead of assisting men in altering their behaviors and to prevent future mistakes, classical conditioning is applied in the form of confinement, and psychological reformation is done with unpredictable outcomes, resulting in unintended consequences."

Gladiator Camp

I already had my preconceptions of what was going to take place in prison from doing my first stretch. I only did 9 months the first time and it was a cakewalk. Everybody had to go through Shelton first; which was classification. That part was always simple unless you got put in the R-units. Those units were less staffed and they didn't allow much recreational time. The first time I got sent up, I was classified into a minimum-security boot camp-like facility and the time passed by quickly. I got into one or two fights but it didn't bother me because I had some patnas in there that had my back. This time, I was on gang file and being sent to a medium security prison up north. It was Clallam Bay but they called it "Gladiator Camp" because of the ruckus that went on there. I heard this was the place that they sent all of the "Thunder-Cats" who were notably gang-affiliated or got into trouble in other facilities. I heard a lot of stories about the Bay but it didn't bother me. I felt like I had to have at least a couple of homies up there. I'd never been to a medium-security prison before. Even in juvenile, I was sent to a minimum-security facility or a camp. I was with the big boys now.

I went to the Bay and the end of 2002. My first day was my worst day. I mean, I didn't expect to have a glorious time in the joint but I was determined to make the best of it. Remember, I was on gang file. During classification they tried their best to house me in a unit with some of my allies to protect me from harm or causing harm. The Department of Corrections did this without questioning the inmate in which they were classifying. They use police intel, court documents, and other anonymous sources. For some reason they classified me with the Bloods. I remembered that my case documents noted Mike Huntley saying that I was Blood affiliated. I was cool with *some* Bloods, but only the ones from my city. I was a Gangster Disciple. When I got to the Bay, I was placed in a unit that mostly consisted of Bloods. I mean, I knew a few of them from the town and others I had heard about, but none of them were my homeboys. I didn't feel like I was in danger but I was definitely out of my comfort zone.

I didn't blend in well at all. My first day in the yard, I saw a couple of my homeboys by the basketball court and I went over to say what's up. The one that I knew the best was my patna Snoop-Ru. His real name was Mario. We both grew up in the CD and even played little league basketball together. He introduced me to a couple of his Blood homies and everything seemed to be cool. He introduced me to a patna of his named Cujo. Cujo was a Blood out of Tacoma. I went to shake his hand

and dude seemed hesitant, like he didn't want to shake my hand. I didn't think anything of it at the time. Around this time, cigarettes were on their way to being banned in Washington's prisons. So, they were kind of a commodity. Cujo was the only one smoking within the crowd that I was in. After I chopped it up with a few of Snoop's patnas, I went to Cujo and asked him for a cigarette. He gave me a mean stare and said, "Fuck you, Blood! Get the fuck out my face before I spit on you! I don't know you, nigga!" He then, cleared his throat like he was gonna hawk a loogie. Without any hesitation, I took off on him! A fight in the yard was not a rare scene but they never lasted long. If cats wanted to fight, they usually planned it in a particular area where there was very little audience, no cameras, and no staff present. I hit this nigga so quick and hard that he immediately dropped to the ground! I continued to pound him until the guards came and grabbed me off of him. If I hadn't punched Cujo when I did, I would've had a negative label or looked at as a punk. I would've lost respect before I had a chance to gain any. I had a short stretch but I wasn't gonna make it too difficult. The guards broke up the fight, or got me off of him, because I was literally pounding him! They sent us both to the hole.

    The other Bloods knew the rules of respect and engagement and didn't stop the fight. Also, they didn't want to get jumped on by the guards or have them thinking they were a part of the fight. They just stood there and watched. Later, I found out that they were upset with me for how I handled it. They weren't mad that I jumped on Cujo; but they weren't too happy with the way Cujo came at me either. They were upset because once I hit him and he was down, I continued to well on him. I didn't give a fuck at that point.

I got 10 days in the hole but they didn't take any good time from me. While I was in there, I just slept, read, and exercised. I did a lot of thinking and writing. The only person that I wrote was my mother. I didn't like calling Tyree too often because I didn't want to know what was going on in the street. I missed my son. I missed him so much that I couldn't even talk to him because of the hurt it would cause. In my writings, I began making plans for my life for when I got out. I promised to leave the game alone but I knew that I had some unfinished business to handle once I got out. I knew that I had another hustle run in me. I wanted to try to go to school for something or find a good job. I also wanted to take care of Mike Huntley. I planned to put as much effort as needed into reevaluating my life and living differently once I was released, but I couldn't get the mindset of being a gangster out of me. I wanted to change and I knew that I had it in me, but everything I knew was about that life. If I knew you, and you weren't about what I was about, then our interactions wouldn't last long. I knew that this had to have been a problem.

They gave people in the hole one hour of recreational time per day, in an isolated area. I was able to talk to two or three other prisoners who were also in the hole. One of them was one of the Blood's OG's named Pimp. We were talking one day and he found out why I was in the hole. He knew Cujo and told me more about him. I found out that this guy wasn't getting out of prison anytime soon and he didn't give a fuck. Cujo was known for doing a series of drive-by shootings in Tacoma and was serving time for murder one. The authorities knew that he was responsible for, or at least involved in, four other murders, but they only prosecuted him for the murder that they had undeniable evidence to convict him on. I also found out that he was involved in a few shankings in Stafford Creek, and one here at Clallam Bay. Pimp told me to look out for him because he was dangerous. He said, "That little dude ain't nothing to play with. Even his big homies respect him because they know he gets his murder game on. He got some influence with the Blood card and is probably going to be running it one day."

Guards came to get me out of the hole after the ten days were up. I was happy but concerned. I asked the guards if they were sending me back to the same unit. The guard said, "Yup, that's where your classification placed you. So, until some other reason arises, that is where you'll be." I have to admit that I was scared. I wasn't trying to go to that same foul ass spot. Cujo had 40-something years. Therefore, killing me wouldn't have mattered to him. I told the guards, "Fuck that!" and refused to leave my cell. I figured that I had a realistic release date and I wasn't going to let my pride, my gangsta, or Cujo fuck that up.

I stayed in the hole for another 3 months. The guards came back a couple of times to put me back into population, but I refused. All I had to do was say that I was in fear of my life. By saying that, it meant that they had to keep me out of what I considered "harm's way". Solitary wasn't the best place to be. However, the solitude and lack of interaction with other inmates and guards gave me the opportunity to figure out a few things about my life. I read the Bible a few times to get a better understanding of it. I read the Qur'an too. I also read some Buddhist scriptures out of the "Tripitaka" to get in touch with my inner-self and for motivational purposes. I knew that Jesus Christ was my lord and savior but I read other religion's scriptures to find out why they felt differently about Him. I read some books about the Crusades and other Holy Wars that have been going on for eons. I felt that if I was going to spend my time alone, I had to gain some useful knowledge. The most important thing that I reflected on while in solitude was my life and things that transpired due to my actions. I did a lot of shit in my life, but I ended up going to prison for the one thing that I was actually innocent of. I wasn't even mad at Boog. Someone fed him some bullshit and he ate it. He wasn't the first one to be put in that kind of situation. Mike Huntley was a bitch and he did exactly what bitch niggas do. He believed that I tried to have Boog take him out, so he made the only move he felt could hurt me. Although I buried myself in the Bible, I hadn't worked my way up to forgiveness; at least not in its entirety.

I had about two months left when the guards came to get me. I was going to tell them the same thing I told them whenever they came back to put me in population. However, this time they were transferring me back to Seattle. I had two cases pending and one of the judges wanted to see me in person; Judge Hightower. Judge Hightower was the presiding judge over my DUI case from 1998. I was on probation for it but never showed up to meet with my probation officer (P.O.). As the presiding judge on my case, she was responsible for issuing the warrants for failing to show up to my review hearings. This happened two or three times, then Judge Hightower had enough. She said, "Mr. Lee, your P.O. doesn't want to see you. I am your probation officer now. Each time you miss your review with me, it'll be 30 days jail time." I still paid it no mind. I mean, I complied for the most part by getting a drug and alcohol assessment and participating in treatment, but I would always abort or get kicked out for pissing dirty. This would lead to me missing my review with her and eventually doing 30 days. When she heard that I was in prison for another crime, I guess she put in a request to have me transported to make the court appearance. I knew there were going to be one of two outcomes. Either she was going to violate me, suspend my probation, or give me 90 days jail time to run concurrently with my sentence that I was already serving, or run it consecutively.

I also had a possession case pending in Tukwila that I had to appear for while I was in Seattle. They ended up running everything concurrently. I stalled on them in order to stay in the county jail until my time was up. Judge Hightower held no sanctions nor did she suspend my sentence. She said, "I have no idea what you've gotten yourself into, Mr. Lee. But you go ahead and finish your jail time and come see me when you're released." I thought to myself, "Shit...I would've rather done an additional 90 days than to have to go back and see her ass."

I was housed in the Regional Justice Center for a month until my release. It was another hell hole of a county jail, except it was cleaner. The difference between county jail and prison is that there were things to do. In county, you just sat there in the tank all day. Even while I was in solitary, I had access to certain materials and went outside once a day. There were a lot of fights in county jail that weren't always in the open too. I ran into a couple of dudes that I had beef with on the streets. I was glad we were in the county. If we were on the streets, it would've been a shootout rather than a fight. I mean, I was a shooter too, but only when it was necessary. I had no problem with fighting. I felt comfortable with my skills as a fighter because it was more of an even playing field. I've been in many fights before and only lost a couple. This was mainly due to me being way smaller, being too loaded, or outnumbered; but I always got back at niggas.

I was hearing good things about my brother while I was down. I heard that he and his crew were actually running things in the hood. Tyree made a couple of power moves which placed him and his crew in a good position. Word was that he was showing cats a lot of love instead of going hard on them. Tyree felt like he did what he had to do to get to the top of his game. But once he got there, he showed the hood love! He even expanded his crew and had a couple of other cats rocking with him. I heard that he was rocking with this guy named Mello. I knew Mello when he was a younger dude. He was actually my patna's nephew. I grew up with his uncle and played little league ball with him. Mello had grown into a real grimy teenager who had a mean hustle. He embodied the role of a gangster that other cats could never live up to. Mello was clearly the product of watching too many gangster flicks. But I liked Mello. My younger brother, Thomas, started hanging around Tyree more and was starting to do his thing too. Tyree and Thomas had always been close since they both shared the middle child spot. Tyree even taught Thomas how to fight when he was younger and he developed a mean right hand. Thomas built a reputation for knocking dudes out over minor disputes.

Dank and 50 were still around too. Dank was building with Tyree and even recruited his own little subgroup of hustlers. They were more like groupies who loved fucking with Dank for the notoriety and protection. Nobody was gonna fuck with you if you got down with Tyree or Dank. 50 still came around but had become more of a loaner. He wasn't into meeting new people that much and was kinda antisocial. He didn't have a crew but he still hustled. Dank and 50 had just recently done some time in the pen too, but they got released way before I did. I talked to Tyree over the phone about what was going on in the hood and how my son was growing. I wasn't tripping or emotional over not seeing him. As a matter of fact, I wouldn't let anyone bring him to see me. Tyree and my mom offered to bring him but I wasn't up for it. They even tried to bring him to the county to see me but I refused that too. I had a reasonable release date and I didn't want to see my son in a visiting room or behind a glass window. That was one thing that I was never going to do if I didn't have to. That might've broken me.

Tyree also gave me the rundown on how reckless my baby momma was acting in the streets. He told me that she was really out there. He said that she was running around with her step-sister doing the most; popping pills, snorting coke, clubbing, and doing all the other shit she had prided herself on not doing. It was more of a shock than anything to me. Yeah, I was hurt. That's only because deep down in my heart, I might've wanted things to work out between us when I got out. I didn't wanna believe a word of what he was telling me. I knew Tyree never really liked Alicia, but he accepted her because she was my girl and the mother of his only nephew. I knew Tyree was telling the truth because he wouldn't slander the broad just for fun. I heard from a couple of other people who were running in and out of the county about her being around places that enabled those kind of activities. I figured that she was trying her best to get back at me. I wrote her twice and she wrote back once. She wrote back talking about how she was getting money, how niggas were taking care of her, and that she had a few trick daddies. By then, I didn't give a fuck. I wrote back and told her to shoot some change on my books, but didn't hear anything back from her. I figured that she could've at least looked out for her son's father, who took care of both of them while we were together. Shit, I was in a tight spot. She should've been the first one to break bread, especially, if she had it.

    I dealt with the heartbreak of my son's mom becoming a tramp while I was in solitude. I read some of Ice Berg Slim's books and fell in love with his book "Pimp". I focused on the part when he was in prison and an older cat was telling him about "iron-cladding" his feelings. It was basically a metaphorical way to help young brothas deal with their emotions that they claimed to not have. The passage meant a lot more to me than what was said. Other people read the book and thought about pimping or something of that nature and lifestyle. I read it and realized that I had to think bigger in order to build my dreams off of motivation and determination, and leave my feelings and emotions far behind. I didn't care about what Alicia was doing with herself. I knew Lil Ty was straight because Tyree told me that whenever she went out, she would drop him off to him or my mom. That settled me and I immediately continued my positive thinking.

"Can we continue to call these criminal institutions "rehabilitation or correctional facilities", with the growing rate of recidivism? Most men who go through the criminal justice system for the first time will find themselves revisiting within a year or so. Where is the regiment for rehabilitation? What is being corrected? When you put these men, who all have behavioral issues, in the same spot where they outnumber authority, how will they engage in altering their behaviors to become productive members of society?"

Real Life

I got out of jail in the spring of 2004. My brother came to pick me up. He had blunts and Henny of course. I dug right into my old addict behaviors. I had sworn off drugs and alcohol while I was locked up but it was right there in front of my face. I didn't even think twice about it. We blew dro, sipped Henny, and talked about what was going on in the hood the entire way home. He told me about his crew and what they were doing. I was tripping on how my little brother had expanded his game. He became a real boss in the streets. Some of the OG's that I was locked up with said that they heard he was doing big things, but I didn't believe it until I saw it for myself. I was proud of him!

My first order of business was to get fitted and cleaned up. We went by the barbershop and some of the homies were there to welcome me home! They were treating me like I had been stretched out for years. I was like, "Damn ya'll! I only did 14 months!" Preston, who had known me my entire life and kind of mentored us from time to time said, "I know, Young Playa. But you did the time and you didn't tell. Everyone knew you were innocent and

Boog was on some bitch shit. You handled that and did your time like a soldier. Real niggas will always respect that." After getting cleaned up, we went by a few other spots to visit some peeps while my brother made a few joogs. I'd been out since 8 o'clock in the morning. I decided to call Alicia around 3:30 – 4:00 P.M. When I talked to her, she was mad that it took so long for me to call. I didn't pay her any mind. I told her to bring my son to me and of course she made it difficult. She claimed that she didn't have a ride, but I didn't believe her. I told her ass that I didn't have one either and I hung up. I went to see my mom and little brothers later on that night and ended up spending the night over there. Mom moved to the west side of town and that's where I was addressed. My D.O.C. officer was also located on that side of town and I had to see her first thing in the morning.

    The next day, I met with my D.O.C. officer and found out that it wasn't going to be easy to stay out of jail unless I tried. I had to report to her once a week until I found a job and I was going to be U.A.'d frequently. I also had to pay restitution. My D.O.C. officer was a woman named Ms. Crawford and she didn't play any games! She didn't care if I claimed that I was innocent of the charges. She let it be known that her job was to monitor my actions and to utilize an aggressive form of supervision. She told me that I was classified as a gang member with a high propensity of reoffending. I didn't like her and I knew that she had me all wrong. I got back to the block and started pumping again, immediately. I ran into a few of my homies and chopped it up with them for a second, but I stayed on the grind.

    I started drinking again but I kind of felt like I had it under control. I had to get a drug and alcohol assessment due to the D.U.I. case I caught a while ago, and D.O.C. wanted me to get one, too. Early one morning, I showed up for an assessment after a night of hard drinking, and they smelled it on me. The lady kicked me out and sent me back to D.O.C. When I got there, I told her about the night before and how it wasn't a problem. She actually gave me a pass on that one but I knew that I didn't have any more.

I continued to drink but I was in denial, which made things a lot worse. I had a few chicks that I would hang out with because I didn't like to drink alone. Drinking alone made me depressed and I'd start feeling sorry for myself and my situation. I knew that if I got drunk with the homies, I'd end up doing something stupid and end up back in jail. I went the DSHS office to schedule a drug and alcohol assessment but they said they were behind on paperwork. Although I was on D.O.C. supervision, I was still on probation with Judge Hightower. She still wanted me to finish treatment for the D.U.I. charge that I caught years back. DSHS set up an appointment for an assessment about a month out. This meant that I was going to continue my drinking and become more inundated in my miserable alcoholic state.

I had been out of jail for about a month when I came across my next life-changing event. I was drunk as shit while downtown one night trying to hustle. I had a gun on me for some reason. My little homie sold it to me for dirt cheap and I couldn't pass it up. I was in Pioneer Square by the nightclubs and saw some dudes choppin it up in the parking lot near the alley. I walked up to them and asked if any of them wanted to buy some weed. They looked at each other and one of them said, "Yeah, whachu got?" I reached into my pocket and pulled out about a half ounce bagged up when I felt one of them punch me in the back of my head. I dropped to the ground and felt someone kick me in my ribs. I rolled over and popped up. I was dazed but I was ready to fuck someone up. I said, "What's wrong with y'all? Which one of you pussies stole on me?" They started to circle around me. There were about four or five of them from what I remember. It looked like they were going to try to jump me and jack me for my weed, so I was looking for a way to run up out of there because I was outnumbered. I remember getting enraged once I remembered that I had a gun on me. I was drunk but I don't know how I forgot? They were literally fucked and had no idea! I didn't know which one of them actually punched or kicked me, but they *all* were going to pay for it! I pulled the gun out of my pants and they started to run towards the alley behind the club. I gave chase and fired all six shots from the revolver. I saw two of them drop so I figured that they were hit. Afterwards, I sprinted in the opposite direction. As I was running towards the pier, I was banging the pistol against the ground and breaking it into pieces. As I ran along the pier, I threw the gun parts into the sound. Then I ran up the block and hopped into a cab.

    I stayed at my homeboy Resin's house for the next four days because I was scared to go home. The next night, I saw the incident on the news and it said two dudes were shot downtown and both were in serious, but not life threatening condition. I was relieved that I hadn't killed anyone. I felt bad about it, but I truly felt like they deserved to get hurt. They were lucky that they didn't get murked! Maybe next time they'll think before trying to jump on someone.

I missed my appointment with my D.O.C. officer and knew that there would be a warrant issued for my arrest. I hit the block for a couple more days before I went home. I lost my cellphone while I was running from the scene, the week before. When I got home, my mom said that my D.O.C. officer stopped by. It was late at night by then. So, I told her I would go see her in the morning.

I went to see my D.O.C. officer the next morning and was immediately arrested. I was violated for missing my appointment the previous week and for pissing dirty. I had to do 30 days, so they sent me back to Clallam Bay for 3 weeks first. This was a huge inconvenience. I had been out of jail for less than two months and I was already back! I was really down on myself. I planned on doing so much better and was disappointed by my actions. Another thing that sucked was not being able to be classified; which meant that I had to do my 3 weeks in solitary. I had a lot of time to beat up on myself and I experienced a lot of negative thinking.

After three weeks, I was brought back to the county jail for my D.O.C. hearing. I plead guilty to all of her accusations so that I could be released with no further pending issues. I had about three more days of jail time to serve when the detectives came to see me. I figured this might've been an issue that I had to face, so I properly prepared for it. When the shooting incident occurred, I had my hair in an afro and didn't have much facial hair because I had recently gotten trimmed up. I hadn't shaved since my arrest and my hair was now braided. Detectives came and talked to me for about 30 minutes about what was going on in the hood. I didn't respond much because I knew that they were fishing. They also talked about my case with Boog and Mike. They said that they knew that I was innocent and that I was being railroaded. That was the only thing that I agreed with. Then they asked about the shooting and where I was during this time. I told them I didn't know about any shooting, especially, the one that they were referring to. They said that I matched a description, they had a witness, and they could place me near the scene of the crime. That's when I asked for a lawyer.

They asked if I would participate in a lineup and I refused. My lawyer arrived and he felt like if I didn't have anything to hide then I should do the lineup. I didn't want him to lose confidence in me, so I did it. I figured that I had changed my appearance enough. Plus, it was dark outside on the night in question. I passed the lineup because their witness couldn't identify me.

I got out of jail on a Thursday and had another appointment for a drug and alcohol assessment that my D.O.C. officer set up for the next day, since I was incarcerated during my last one. I got up early in the morning and attended the assessment. For the first time, I answered all of the questions truthfully. I felt like I had nothing to lose this time. I thought to myself, "Fuck it. What's the worst thing that could happen?" I had somewhat of a long history of alcohol abuse for my young age and had been kicked out of outpatient treatment three times. So, the drug and alcohol counselor recommended inpatient treatment.

I knew that I was going to have to go to inpatient soon but I didn't have a date set yet. The lady from the assessment agency said that they would call me when they had a spot ready. I called my D.O.C. officer to let her know what was going on and she requested that I come see her the day before I went in. I don't know why I decided to be truthful now, but I was. I told her, "Naw, Ms. Crawford. I don't think I'm going to do that, and I'm going to tell you why. I'm an alcoholic who is in need of help. Plus, I have a series of other issues that I need to address. I'm going to drink my ass off until they call me and hopefully when they do call, I'll still be alive. But when they call, I'm going. The only thing that's going to stop me from going this time is if you send me to jail again. And the only way I can prevent you from doing that is by staying the hell away from you until I get to treatment." She remained adamant about me coming to see her before treatment and threatened more violations, but I was over her and the whole system at that point. I chose to play the blame game with everyone who opposed me and how I felt. I had an appointment to get an assessment before my D.O.C. officer violated me the first time. I missed the appointment and was still in active addiction because of that. I knew that there was more to it, but I felt right in believing that and blaming her. But I knew that I couldn't go home.

The next few days were a blur to me. I was under the influence all of the time. I spent a little time with Ty and Alicia so that I could let her know what was going on in my life, but she wasn't feeling me. She was giving me bullshit about being a bad father and how I'd hardly spent any time with Ty since I'd been out. I told her that I had issues to deal with and this was going to be good for me. However, she remained pessimistic about me and my situation. I knew she wouldn't understand. Her mother was an addict for most of her life so she had little belief in addicts. I knew Alicia had internal issues but they weren't my problems or for me to fix. Her problems mixed with the ones I had of my own did not mix. I had a crazy thought of us being together one day to raise our son and possibly have more children, but I knew that this would never be. It wasn't because she had been somewhat of a whore while I was locked up, or because she didn't look out for me when I needed her the most. It was because I knew that we would never see eye-to-eye. If any kind of relationship would've continued, I would've been miserable due to her crazy beliefs and her perception of people. I mean...she even had an issue with the type of relationship that I had with my mom! She despised the relationship that I had with my mom because she didn't have a similar type of relationship with hers. I would've been a fool to think that we could've ever been together again. When I went to treatment, I left Alicia for good.

"If you hold men to the highest standard of accountability, they will rise to the occasion because they can. If you allow men to act like adolescents they will oblige you..."

New Leaf

By the time I got the call that a spot was available for treatment, I was a mess. I managed to stay loaded the entire time before I entered detox. I was still hustling but I was reckless. I even went to Downtown Seattle, the hottest area in the city, to sell dope. I knew it was a high-risk situation, but I wanted to make sure I got rid of all of my goods before I went in. I was begging for trouble! I went home the night before and called my Aunt Lisa and asked her to give me a ride to detox in the morning.

I was hung over when she picked me up the next morning and she wouldn't allow me to get a drink. She took me to eat breakfast before dropping me off. My aunt and I had a long talk on the way to detox. My Aunt Lisa was a college-educated woman and was living a successful life. She was single, had no kids, and truly wanted the best for her nephews. I know that if I ever needed anything, she would do whatever she could to see that it got done. She bailed me out of jail before when I was broke, helped me buy a car when I was short on money, helped pay for my lawyer, and she really looked out for Lil Ty when I was locked up. I had a high level of appreciation, love, and respect for her. She asked me, "Ty, how did things get so bad with this drinking and drugging?" I told her, "I don't know, Auntie. I just need to clear my mind before I start to make any plans." Aunt Lisa said, "Ty, you're very intelligent. I really think that you should consider going back to school. Your intelligence, street savvy, and experiences are enough to make you a very good drug and alcohol counselor." She mentioned this because when I was younger, I said that counseling was something that I wanted to do because I felt like the drug counselors that I encountered in my life were full of shit and had no real passion for their clients or the field. I've always had this idea in the back of my mind but I never knew what it was going to take to get me there or if I would ever have the time, patience, or opportunity to pursue it. I told her that it was definitely something to think about while I evaluated other areas of my life that needed major reconstruction. I had to go to detox for 5 days before entering the treatment facility.

Detox was cool because I got a chance to get some real rest. I'd been couch surfing because I hadn't established any kind of housing when I got out of jail. I was staying between my mom's, my brother's, and various chick's houses. I got a check-up while I was in detox. This was something that I hadn't done in years. The check-up consisted of a physical, HIV test, and an STD screening. I never had an HIV test before and it was some scary shit! Back then, it took a couple of days to get the results, so I spent the next couple of days thinking about all of the unprotected sex and one night stands that I had in the past. The test came back negative but I tested positive for gonorrhea. I was actually relieved it was just that. The only frightening thing about it was that I didn't know which female I contracted it from or who I might've given it to. I realized that I didn't want to have that kind of fear again and I swore off meaningless sex.

    I got to treatment a week later and immediately started to question its purpose. I was at a place called the Thunderbird. It was located in South Seattle in a remote location and I had to do at least 30 days. I was fed a bunch of information that didn't apply to me but I was told to internalize it anyway. I have to admit that I didn't go to treatment to get clean. I was actually hiding out from D.O.C. I felt that if I did this, Ms. Crawford might not violate me once I got out.

    The first day there, my counselor asked if I was on any kind of probation or supervision. When I said "Yeah", he asked if he could call my probation officer. I told him no because I missed my last appointment and she would probably send someone to come and get me. The counselor informed me that the D.O.C. couldn't come to get me because there were federal laws prohibiting that from happening.

He said, "Unless you're wanted for a capital or federal crime, they can't come here and get you. Now sit your ass down until something clicks." It was a weight lifted off of my shoulders and I was able to relax.

I was, by far, the youngest dude in the treatment facility. I was surrounded by a bunch of old-timers who had obviously been around the ringer. They mostly consisted of crack-heads, dope fiends, and stone-cold alcoholics. I was a pothead who abused alcohol; so I thought. I felt like I didn't fit in and treated this experience with an uncertainty. I mean…I respected the process and the purpose of it. I just felt like my habit hadn't reached that level yet. I was in group one day, and the term "disease concept" kept getting thrown around. I didn't believe addiction was a disease. My intelligence knew exactly what a disease was and what it consisted. To me, an addiction was more like a character defect or a habit in its worst form. I honestly believed this until I got my coattail pulled by an older dude in the group one day. This cat told me, "Don't be arrogant to your ignorance of this disease. I was just like you when I was your age and never had the opportunity that you have right now. I promise you. If you don't get this shit now, it WILL get worse. You will be just like us in 15-20 years, if not sooner." He jokingly added, "This is your life Charlie Brown." I argued with him for a minute and the counselor let us go at it for a minute. I came at him with my smarts and defined the characteristics of a disease. I talked about viruses, bacteria, and how pathogens enter our system without any genetic pathway. He said, "Look, youngin. You seem smart but you're very naïve. It doesn't take a lot of smarts to figure it out. Once you believe this is a disease you might get this. Any disease you get, the medicine or remedy comes in the form of a treatment. Most of us don't get this chance. This is TREATMENT, young nigga! You better get you some!" I understood what he was saying, but my pride wouldn't let me agree. I gracefully bowed out of the discussion because no one else in the group agreed with me. I must've been wrong but I didn't understand how?

After the group was over, I asked the counselor, "Dude, why'd you let us continue for so long?" He said, "Because it would've been harmful to not let you endure that therapeutic process. It was a discussion that needed to happen. If I told you that this was a disease, you would've believed me and not questioned it. But when it came from someone who has the disease and is currently fighting it, you disagree? You're perception is all wrong, young brother. You need to wake up and look at what you've been questioning your whole life. You're shooting the messenger and disregarding the message."

I had my moment of clarity about two weeks into treatment. I received a new roommate because my other one left treatment against his counselor's advice. My new roommate was a middle-aged brother named Reuben. Reuben was an old pimp and long-time heroin addict. He spent his first couple of days sleeping because he just came off of a run. We used to talk at night while we were in the TV room. He was an old acquaintance of my dad and had taken a liking to me because he said that he saw potential in me. I became a very angry and an impatient person by this time. I was mad at the situation that I found myself in. I was angry at the system that kept me in this current state. However, I was really mad at myself because I felt like I was a failure. I would never tell anyone else this because of my pride. But I could never lie to myself. I knew that I had what it took for me to snap back but I was morally fatigued. I needed a better understanding of life and was willing to open myself up to the advice being given by the counseling staff and other patients. I started looking for inspiration in other people's stories and began seeing what lessons could be learned. I believe this is when I decided to give into the program.

One night, Reuben and I were discussing what we had been through and how it put us in our current situations. I remember saying sarcastically, "So what? We come here, listen to a couple of people tell us we're addicts for a few weeks, divulge our true feelings, listen to some literature, and then everything will be okay?" Reuben always had something witty to say whenever I was being sarcastic. His response would be like a screwball pitch or a change-up. Reuben had a high level of intelligence even though he dropped out of school in the 7th grade. He was street smart and had experienced a lot. Reuben spent a lot of time in prison and had been using heroin since the 70's. He met some very infamous people, traveled all over the country while pimping, and was game tight when it came to communication with others. He was very persuasive; something you had to be if you were going to be a pimp. When I made these sarcastic remarks, Reuben sat up on the edge of his chair and said, "Shit, it can't get much worse." I slept on that.

We had these daily AA/NA meetings that people from the outside would sometimes attend. Sometimes people who were in the program would invite friends and family members to attend and would use this as a time for visits. I never invited anyone. I decided that this was my program and I didn't want to burden anyone with my issues. This was something that I had to do on my own. Honestly, I didn't know how I was going to remain clean and sober once I was released from treatment. I knew it would take some hard work and re-strategizing of my life. I was up for it.

I had a court date with Judge Hightower a week before I was to be released. My brother came and picked me up. He was waiting in front of the treatment facility with his music blaring and puffin on a blunt. I hopped into the car and chewed him out about it. He didn't give a fuck. He said, "Nigga, I ain't in treatment! And you don't have to worry about nothing unless you hit this blunt." I was upset but I got over it as we headed downtown.

The courtroom was semi-full when we got there. I looked at the docket and saw that I was 10th on the list. I knew that meant we were gonna be there for at least a half hour before my case was heard. When Judge Hightower came out of her chambers, she looked at the docket and then out into gallery. She looked directly at me and told her clerk, "Let's handle Mr. Lee's case first." I thought to myself, "Aw, shit!" Tyree laughed because he knew our history and he was high as a kite. The Judge said, "Okay, Mr. Lee. The last time that you were here you were in prison serving time for another offense. Now that you're out, what have you been doing with yourself?" I said, "Your Honor, I've been re-evaluating my life and I have entered inpatient treatment earlier this month. I should be done in a week or so. Here are the necessary documents from the clinical supervisor at the facility that I'm at, along with papers from my D.O.C. officer that states that I am in compliance." The clerk handed her the papers and she looked over them carefully. She looked up and said, "Well Mr. Lee. We have been dealing with this case for some time now. I am going to let you complete your treatment because it seems like you're doing well. When you are done, have the facility send the necessary paperwork to the department of licensing and then you will be able to start the process of getting your driver's license reinstated. Good luck, Mr. Lee. And I don't want to see you under these circumstances again." I said, "Thanks." Tyree was impressed with the way that I handled my business with her. He heard me talk about the way things usually went whenever I saw her. Shit, I actually had to sneak out of the courtroom once to keep myself from being detained. But it looked like that chapter of my life was over. I felt like I had a new lease on my freedom and I actually cared. No more arrest warrants being issued by Judge Hightower. Things like this motivated me to remain clean and sober.

On our way back to the treatment facility, Tyree told me about what dudes were saying about me in the hood. Some people said that I had fallen off and started smoking crack, others thought that I went crazy, and some were just saying the truth; that I was a stone cold alcoholic and was at the point of no return. I guess they were thinking that I was one step away from being the next whino in front of the liquor store begging for change? They had me fucked up. Tyree said that he and the ones that mattered knew the truth. He said that he could only straighten out so many of them without telling them any of my business. I said, "Go ahead and tell them the truth. Tell them I'm an alcoholic and I'm in treatment. There's no reason for me to run from the truth." My little brother looked at me and told me that he was proud of me. It felt good to hear that from him.

Although, there were many people who were waiting on my downfall, he was one of the few who had faith in me. When I got back to the treatment facility, they immediately gave me a urine test because I smelled like weed from being in the car with Tyree. I told them that my ride was smoking and that they could run any test they wanted on me. I knew that I wasn't dirty.

I had a couple of days left in treatment and was starting to build an exit strategy. I knew that the only stable place that I could stay at was my mom's house. My mom and Craig were only smoking weed and drinking, occasionally. They both worked and were doing much better by then. I was happy for them. I knew that I had a hard road ahead of me and it wasn't going to be easy. The day before I was discharged, I had to do a "first step". This was a detailed description of my life, and how drugs and alcohol impacted and destroyed my life. I feared this because I was going to have to tell the truth. My pride and dignity had always protected me from my fears. Letting my guard down was something that I wasn't used to. It wasn't because I became an alcoholic/addict or that I feared being judged. And it surely wasn't because I caused harm to others or committed acts that landed me in jail. I heard others do their first step and it was mainly comprised of shame and all of the destruction they caused their loved ones. I knew that some people's stories were much more fucked up than mine. My biggest disappointment was that I contributed to my mother's addiction. I loved her. And after being clean for a certain amount of time, I had a chance to reflect on my own wrongdoings. This was the only time that I truly felt like a piece of shit. I knew that she was in a bad place and I didn't do anything to help. I felt bad for deceiving my grandmother for all of those years. I didn't feel bad for the niggas I shot, the people that I robbed, or the ones that I decided to put hands on. I felt that those actions were necessary and it was part of the game we played. I never gave it to anyone who didn't deserve it. I don't think the people that robbed, shot, and put hands on me felt any remorse either? This is something that I would learn to understand and work on later in life. For now, I had to focus on coming to terms with my wrongs and begin to grow. I knew that bringing harm to others was immoral in God's eyes. And I felt like He was the only one that I would have to answer to for that. When that day came, my goofy ass would probably still try to justify my actions. But I had no answer for contributing to my mother's addiction or lying to my God-fearing grandmother. They loved me unconditionally.

    I got out of treatment and went directly to my D.O.C. officer. I didn't have an appointment or anything. I just felt like I had to report to her before I tried to do anything else. When I got there, it looked like she'd been waiting on me. I didn't know if I was going to be arrested or violated. She said, "Hey, Mr. Lee. I got a call from your treatment facility and they said that you made good progress while there." I said, "Yeah, I didn't have much of a choice." She said, "Now, you know that you were supposed to meet with me before you went in. I was supposed to issue a warrant for your arrest but since I received a call from your counselor at the Thunderbird informing me of your whereabouts, I didn't issue one. But that still wasn't an excuse for you to miss our appointment." I told her the truth. I told her, "I knew that I was going to inpatient and I was in a bad place in the weeks leading up to that day. I hope you can understand that." She had me take a urine test. She also let me know that I couldn't have any more missed appointments or I would be violated again. She didn't have to tell me that twice. I wasn't trying to go back to jail.

I was in the CD and called my homie Clown to see if he could give me a ride home. He said yeah, but I had to meet him at a club called Larry's in downtown. I just got out of treatment and had only been clean and sober for about a month. I was a little passive-aggressive but was able to stabilize myself and remain humble. I was money motivated but I didn't wanna do anything to jeopardize my freedom, or my newly found sobriety.

I wasn't quite ready for the club scene and felt very uncomfortable there. Back when I used to go to clubs, I was usually the one getting crunk, hollering at chicks all night long, and eventually leaving with one. Tonight was different. I wasn't drunk or high and was very observant of my surroundings. I knew that I was in a cool spot and I had a couple of my patnas there with me, but I still had some kind of worry in me. I still can't explain it to this day.

I was there for about an hour when I saw her. I was sitting down and she was walking through the dance floor. She was sexy and she caught me looking at her. We made eye contact for about 5 seconds before I thought "fuck it" and walked her way. I've never been a dancer, especially, in the clubs. I mean…I would boogie and two-step and shit, but I was never the "middle of the dance floor" type of dude. I walked over to her and we started dancing. She was a Native-mixed, with long brown hair and blue eyes. We danced through two songs before I decide to have a seat. She said, "What? You don't wanna dance with me no more?" I said, "Of course I do, Ma. You're very cute but my feet are killing me. You wanna go have a seat?" She said yeah, so we went to have a seat and conversed for a few minutes before exchanging numbers. Her name was Christine.

Before I left treatment, my counselor told me that I also had to do some outpatient. I was cool with handling any and all of my legal obligations in order to stay in compliance with D.O.C. and Judge Hightower. Attending outpatient was actually killing two birds with one stone. I was able to satisfy both courts while staying on track to get my driver's license back. This time around, outpatient wasn't so bad because I completed inpatient first. I was only there for two hours, a couple of times a week. It was highly manageable and gave me a chance to handle other things in my life. I had a case manager named Kim. He was a White guy with a woman's name. I didn't know if it was a nickname or if it was short for something? He was very easy-going and laid back. He said that as long as I came to my groups and gave him clean U.A.'s, I wouldn't have any problems. He said that he would send monthly compliance letters to the judge and my D.O.C. officer. After three months, he would send the paperwork to lift the hold on my driver's license. I was cool with it.

Another one of my requirements was to attend three AA/NA meetings a week and get a slip signed. I never liked the idea of Alcoholics Anonymous. I mean, I understood the meaning of it and why people went. But I didn't like the dynamics of some of the meetings that I've been to in the past. Sometimes, when I went to a meeting I would share if I was in a good mood or just felt like sharing, but only on rare occasions. Whenever I got called on, I would pass because I didn't like being put on the spot. Most of the meetings that I went to were in the hood. It was a convenient way of getting my meeting slips signed while I was in the area making joogs. After a while, I started to notice that nearly everyone was in the same boat and externally motivated. They weren't there to get or stay clean and sober. They all had legal obligations and were there for convenience. I knew that I was contradicting my own reasoning.

I started looking for the people who attended AA/NA meetings because they wanted to be there and not because they had to be there. I wanted to know what their motivation was and what they got from these meetings. Another thing that I hated about these meetings in the hood were the old-timers. These were dudes who had decades of clean and sober time and used it as weight to shove around. They did more harm than anything by bragging about how much clean time they had. I was talking to an old-timer once and he asked me, "How old are you?" I told him that I was 25 years old. He responded, "Youngin, I got more time clean and sober than you have living." It was a stupid response and uncalled for. Shit, I don't even know why he asked me my age if that was gonna be his response? I heard a guy tell another young brotha, "I done probably spilled more alcohol than you've drank." I thought, "Where's the glory in that? And how is that supposed to inspire someone who is trying to get clean and sober or motivate them to keep coming back?" I knew that I had it in my mind that I wanted long-term sobriety and didn't want to be like these old folks. I also didn't want my mind trying to find a reason not to believe in the program. I wasn't trying to put myself in a situation that would lead me to think negatively about this entire process. I wanted to have faith in the program but these old fuckers gave me doubt!

I was speaking to my case manager, Kim, about these types of issues that I was experiencing in my meetings. Kim asked me, "What meetings have you been going to?" When I told him where, he said, "T, you've got to expand yourself and branch out to other meetings. You're gonna get the same shit if you go to the same meetings. There are meetings all over, every day, and at every hour." He gave me a booklet that showed the times and places where meetings were held in the entire Seattle area. I wasn't afraid of branching out. Kim said, "If you're gonna get this, you have to want it! But first, you have to figure out why you want it and let that be your motivation." I thought about what Kim said and gave it some deep thought. Kim also told me that I had to get a sponsor. A sponsor was a person who worked with people who were in different stages of their recovery and gave extra support. One of their main purposes is to interpret the literature from the Alcoholics Anonymous book. I never had a sponsor before because I was never committed to staying clean and sober. I also gave this some deep thought and tried to imagine what having a sponsor would be like? I knew that he would have to be the complete opposite of what I was used to.

I sought at least two meetings a week outside of my usual area. I went to a few on the eastside that mainly consisted of businessmen/women who would drop in during their lunch break or after work. The shares that people gave were cool but nothing too intriguing or anything that I could relate to. It was way too organized for me. Whenever I went out west for a meeting, the setting was similar to the meetings in the CD. There wasn't much of a difference. As I spread myself around to different meetings, my hunger for long-term sobriety increased. This was because it felt good being clean and sober. I was becoming a more responsible adult. Attending meetings, going to groups, and seeking employment added structure to my life and I felt like I had a purpose. I started to think more about my future and what I wanted my life to be like.

I went to a lunchtime meeting in Ballard a few times because I liked the atmosphere. There wasn't anything spectacular about this meeting except the high level of friendliness. The people there were cool. I opened up and shared about myself, what I had been through, and what I was aiming for in life. Whenever the meetings were over I would usually just get up and leave. I didn't stay and socialize with people because I would usually have shit to do. But after I shared, people wanted to start a conversation with me afterwards. I would stay and chat a little sometimes, but never for too long. I didn't have anything in common with most of these people, except the desire to stop drinking. But, I guess that was enough.

Each time I went to the lunchtime meeting in Ballard, there would be this dude there. He shared sometimes and would always reflect on the importance of values, respect, and self-worth. He was a tall Native-American man with a deep voice. I could tell that he was a fisherman of some sort by the clothes he wore. He didn't speak much to others but he would always congratulate someone when they shared on their clean time. I'd been coming there for a while when I announced that I had one year clean and sober. He came up to me after the meeting and congratulated me. He said, "Good job on your year! Here is your coin!" He handed me a coin that indicated a year of sobriety. Then he asked me, "Now, what's changed?" I said, "What?" He asked me again, but this time a little bit louder, "What has changed?" I thought for a moment before I responded but I couldn't come up with anything. I told him, "I don't know. I gotta think about that one for a minute." I was surprised that I really didn't have an answer for him. I mean, I knew that I felt good. Good enough to not want to drink at this point in my life. He said, "Well, let me know when you want to figure it out."

The next couple of times that I went to the meeting in Ballard, the man wasn't there. I learned that his name was John and he was a frequent member of this group in particular, but he was also present at other groups all over the town. I wanted to know what he meant when he asked me, "What has changed?" I also wanted to know how he could help me figure it out. I found myself coming to these meetings more and more because of the people, the convenience, and the atmosphere. But the main reason that I kept coming after my year of sobriety was to run into John again. When I finally did run into him, he approached me first and said, "I heard that you were looking for me?" I told him that I asked about him. He said, "What does your schedule look like?" I told him that I was free whenever. He said, "Alright, let's go have some coffee."

We went to a nearby coffee shop down the road and talked for a minute about what sobriety meant to him. He said that sobriety was about change. He asked me about myself and who I was. I told him a little about myself but he didn't seem satisfied. He responded and said, "No. I don't want to know about where you're from, what you've been through, or how you feel certain attributes define you. I want to know who Tyrome is. What do your dreams entail? What are your ambitions and motivations? What's in your heart?" John went in deep on me. He knew that this was something that I couldn't answer in one sitting. He changed subjects and focused on behavior and the perception of my behavior. John had a theory that consisted of accountability and behavior. He held men to a high standard. He felt that if you set the bar high, men would achieve that standard; and if you allowed them to act like adolescents, they would. John developed his own way of interpreting life, behavior, and its relevance to addiction. John said, "Tyrome, I know where you come from and what your life consists of. I can also see that this is something you want to do in order to better your life. But what are you willing to give up in order to achieve it? Drugs and alcohol are not the problem. It's the lifestyle, people, and your environment that fosters your addiction." He said, "How do you know that you have a drug and alcohol problem?" I said, "When you can't control it or when you realize it's affecting other areas of your life." He said, "No, it's much simpler than that. You know that you have a drug and alcohol problem when drugs and alcohol causes problems. Look at your first DUI. This wasn't the breaking point. When you decided that you could function while under the influence, that still wasn't a turning point. Your recreational weed smoking had nothing to do with it either. You have to realize that you've always had a predisposition to addiction already within you. And everything about your lifestyle and environment activated your addiction gene. What I want to help you do is learn to suppress that gene by a self-determined behavioral modification, executed at your discretion."

I never believed that addiction was a hereditary symptom that you could inherit. But when I looked at my family tree, I could see it being evident. I asked

John, "So, is it the way I think or my thinking method that will help modify my behavioral methods?" He said, "No. It's changing what you think about how you think. Don't worry. I know some things are better interpreted by actions. I tell you what…let us meet next week after the lunch meeting and further discuss it. We'll take baby steps. We can implement a regiment of behavior modification techniques that coincide with what your life consists of now. If you develop a new perception of life, you'll have no choice but to change your ways."

I thought about my discussion with John. I looked at a number of instances in my life in which I always blamed others instead of looking at the part I played in those circumstances. It was much more than recovering from drugs and alcohol; it was about recovering from a lifestyle. I loved the game. I felt like I was bred to be raised in it. But for some reason, I felt like the game had failed me by allowing me to activate genetic malfunctions that rendered me to be less than a boss. I started looking into my anger. My anger led me into doing things that were uncontrollable at times. I never knew the impact that my anger played in my life and how it fostered resentment. When I met up with John, I told him that's where I wanted to start. He agreed that it was a good place to begin our focus. After we talked for a while, he told me to call him whenever I felt angered and frustrated. He said, "Just hit me before it gets too out of hand at least. Let's learn how to process your feelings first, then we'll discuss the channels we use afterwards." I talked to John a lot over time. I would call him after experiencing a situation where I thought that my anger was getting the best of me. John was a cool guy. He helped me learn things about myself that I never realized. He taught me how to use my anger for good. And it helped me to be able to recognize my true feelings and alter my faulty beliefs.

"I bet you've never realized how much a single incident can impact the masses. A single murder ignited World War I. We put ourselves in a revolving cycle of genocide when we politic our business dwellings with unethical practices. We feel morally obligated to conduct ourselves in a manner that depicts and defines what and where we are at the present time, instead of who we really are as people. The character of our community is made up of the chemistry created. We all have a systematic way of operating."

Tidal Turns and Politics

2005 - 2007

I was chilling at my brother's spot when I learned about a beef going on in the hood between the LP's and Union. My brother wasn't a part of either of the gangs. As a matter of fact, he was cool with people from both sides. The LP's were a gang started up by some of our homies that we grew up with. It was originated by my patna Flames and his younger brothers back when they were hitting bank licks. It started out as a little crew but cats started cliquing in when they saw the money that these cats were making. The tried to stay under the radar when they were pulling licks by not being too flashy, but that didn't work. LP stood for "Low Profile" and these cats were anything but. I was cool with all of them. Even when they became arrogant because of the dough they were having. They were hustlers. But they were also gangsters when it was necessary.

There was a crew from Union who called themselves "Hunnids". Union was a street gang in the CD that had been around for decades and was often referred to as "Union Street Hustlers" (USH). They were probably one of the biggest gangs in Seattle and they were spread all over the place. Union and Deuce 8 were both CD gangs that had been relevant as far back as I could remember. They had members who were dead and gone, some were in prison, and others had fallen off to drugs and shit. There were plenty of active OG's and plenty of up-and-coming members who were eager to display their loyalty. I repped Union for years but had personal allegiances with those that I was close to. I hadn't quite outgrown gangbangin' but I had priorities that I had to tend to other than the block that I claimed. The Hunnids were a new breed of gangsters from Union that consisted of the newer generation. They called their crew "Hunnids" because of the money they were making. This new era felt that you should judge people by the money they had, rather than, personal values and integrity.

Tyree was reppin his own gang, 31st. It was actually the street that we grew up on. My patnas, Love, Hobz, the Big Homie Haze, and I started it when we were younger because we didn't want to be followers like everyone else. We grew a little but didn't expand like the other gangs. We repped Gangster Disciples too but were scrutinized because of how small we were and we didn't have any OG's from our block. This got us some respect but we eventually grew out of it. Love moved away, Haze had a baby and bounced, I started selling dope and took up with my Uncle T.O. from Union, but Hobz stuck around. Tyree started his crew with Love's nephew, Conman. They started reppin it and niggas starting latching on. Tyree never liked being considered the crew's leader. He just felt like everyone had a position to play. His crew respected Hobz as one of the originators because he was the only original member that was still active in the hood and still representin'.

The reason behind the beef cooking was due to a shooting that took place. Tyree's homeboy Mello was shot by the homie Def from Union. These guys were all cool at one point. Def was a little older than us. Tyree linked up with him while I was away. Tyree started buying his work soft and needed someone to help him cook it up. Tyree and his crew weren't into cooking, so he hooked up with Def. I knew how to cook but I had been in and out of jail and treatment for the last couple of years. He needed someone more consistent and reliable. Mello was another young goon that linked up with LP, but his relatives were long-time members and affiliates of Deuce-8. Mello got into an argument with Def at Tyree's trap house and Tyree had to come between them. Mello was much younger than Def, yet, was bigger and physically stronger. Def was a short dude, wasn't much of a fighter, but he's been in heat before. He was known as a shooter and even beat a murder rap back in the day. None of this mattered to Mello.

Coincidentally, Mello and Def ran into each other at the park a couple of days after their altercation at Tyree's spot. Def had Jinx with him but Mello still approached him. I'm not sure what words were exchanged but eventually things got heated. Mello punched Def and dropped him! Def looked at Jinx as if he was supposed to do something. Jinx was also from Union and was a G himself, but he didn't see any reason to jump in at that point. Def was his own gangster, who had words with another man, which resulted in him getting punched. Jinx fell back. Def's ego was crushed and his pride took over. He reached into his pants and pulled out his gun! Mello didn't flinch an inch! He walked up to Def and said, "You pussy nigga. How you gonna pull a gun out on the little homie? I always knew you were soft!" Def pointed the gun at Mello's face. Mello was less than a foot away. Mello said, "Nigga, do something!" really loud and then flinched at him. The gun went off! Def shot Mello in the face! Mello dropped as Jinx and Def fled the scene. Amazingly, Mello got up and fled too. He was about four blocks from Tyree's house. When he got there, his jaw was hanging off his face and blood was gushing out. Tyree got him into his car and sped to the hospital.

Mello survived getting shot in the face. His jaw was wired shut and the bullet was lodged near his temple. The doctors didn't want to take it out in fear of causing further damage. Whatever the case, this sparked the fire that was about to take place in the hood. While Mello was in the hospital, Tyree set out to find Def. He didn't need to hear anyone else's side of the story. All he knew was that Def shot an unarmed Mello in the face. There could be no logical reason for him doing this, he thought. Yeah, he was cool with Def; but Mello was his boy, his little homie, and his protégé. He didn't want answers. He wanted Def's his head!

It was only logical to think that Mello's family members, who were Deuce-8 members, would retaliate against Def, but a lot of them were locked up. It was a known fact that the OG's and shot-callers in the prisons had a strong influence of what went down in the streets. Everyone knew that Def was out of line for shooting Mello. He tried to justify his actions by saying that he warned Mello. He felt that Mello should've backed down when he flashed the gun, but he didn't. As a matter of fact, he dared Def to shoot him! He figured that it was more of Mello's fault since his threat was obliged. The crazy thing that made it even worse was that a majority of the G's from Union was backing Def. This was solely based on loyalty. This was a clear display of unity between gangs but also presented major problems. It didn't matter if Def was wrong. The fact that he was a loyal member from Union meant the rest of the members had to back him. Morality or truth didn't hold any weight in these types of circumstances. The fact that they were in the same outfit made them obligated to ride with him.

These types of politics existed in gangs in and out of prisons. In the most extreme cases, the gang may punish their own, but not to someone who had equity or longevity within the gang. Def was an early member of the Union Street Hustlers and had been reppin the block for most of his life. He put in work, put niggas on, and kept his mouth shut in some dire situations. They owed him too much to let him ride against the Deuce 8's alone if it came down to it.

As far as the Deuce 8's went, it was much more political. Some of the OG's from Deuce 8, Union, and other influential members of prominent gangs, in and out of prison, had many business ventures in play. This inner-neighborhood turf war was nonsense to them. The only time they went to the extreme was against crews from the South End, gangs from other cities, and ones that consisted of other races. Yeah, they understood things went wrong and that Def pulled a foul move. But engaging in an inner-hood war would put a strain or stoppage on their business.

A lot of them felt that since Mello was going to make a full recovery, they should come to some kind of alternate solution that didn't involve violence. Mello wasn't satisfied with this decision. He was gonna ride and wanted other people to fall in line and ride with him! Mello's uncle, RB, was in prison and was also a long-standing member of Deuce 8. He tried to barter with cats but even *he* couldn't get cats to agree to a war. Things were going good money-wise in the streets, cats were doing well, and some of the OG's were even getting out soon. Some of them had kids and loved ones in the streets. They were concerned for them and their fate if war broke out. Others just didn't want a flush of deaths and more young brothas in prison for lengthy sentences. Some of these OG's actually cared about the future generation and opted for an alternate solution.

After being dissatisfied with the OG's from Deuce 8 and their decision to not back him, Mello went on his own rampage. One thing that impressed him was his LP homies and how they stepped up to join him in his carnage. They were nowhere near as deep as the Union crew but they rode with him. He didn't denounce his affiliation with Deuce 8 because it was in his blood to always be allegiant to them. But he did talk shit about certain members on numerous occasions. This eventually caused some of the Deuce 8 members to have animosity with Mello and the rest of the LP's. Before we knew it, there was an inner-hood war between LP, Deuce 8, and Union. My brother was the strongest representative from 31st and he made sure that people knew that. But his loyalty sided with those he fucked with. He and Dank were always loyal to each other first, even though Dank was originally from Deuce 8. Tyree and Dank went all the way back to the fourth grade and their allegiance to one another came before any set they claimed. Tyree was true to Mello, who was also Deuce 8 affiliated, but was a part of the LP crew, too. When Tyree and Dank started putting shit together to make money, Mello was the first to display his loyalty. Tyree and Flames were real tight but it was more like business. Flames, Tyree, and I also went as far back as elementary school too. We used to fight our dogs against each other's when we were kids. Flames repped LP but always kept his mind on making money first. He hated beefs but understood it was necessary sometimes. I was the outlier. I was one of the founding members of 31st, but I was blessed into Disciples by my Uncle Tommy, and made my bones on Union. I still repped Union but I wasn't too affiliated with the new school members. I mean…I knew them and was even cool with most of them, but we had different values and principles. You see…Union was founded on hustling. Everyone from the block associated themselves with getting money and making sure the rest of the members had action at it. It was "street socialism" because everyone had the opportunity to at least get a piece. Shit, if you really needed it then someone would give it to you. The newer generation Union members were also hustlers. But they were more bent on being flashy with their money and stunting on cats…kind of similar to the LP members. This was how the younger crowd displayed their hustle but it also attracted attention. I definitely didn't need that attention. I had a strike against me, a few other points racked up, and I was still on probation with D.O.C.

    Dank got into some shit shortly after the beef started. He got into it with some guy at the club and ended up beating the shit out of dude and his bitch! The only reason why he hit the broad was because she hit him over the head with a bottle while he was pounding the dude. Later on, Dank left the club and the dude rolled up on him again. He started shooting at Dank and he returned fire. While they were having this shootout, a patrol car just happened to roll between them. The dude screeched out while Dank was still returning fire. A couple of Dank's bullets hit the cop's car and then the cop got out and shot Dank. He wasn't critically wounded or anything. But he was facing some serious charges!

    I'd see my brother every time I went to the hood. So, I would usually end up chilling and politicking with Tyree and his crew. Although, I was only a couple of years older than all of them, they looked up to me for advice on how to handle things in their beefs. I was from Union and knew Def and most of the people he ran with, but I wasn't close to them. Even though I was from Union, I only fucked with certain cats. I hated that I never had much advice to give them or the advice that they needed. How could I put it? In the words of Michael Corleone, "I wasn't a wartime consigliere." I didn't do war. If I had a beef, it was between me and that person. I was known for handling shit one-on-one and putting in work. In the past, they mistook my actions as that of a soldier, when I was actually more of a goon. I did advise them to always focus on a solution or some kind of end game. I feared that someone was going to end up badly injured, dead, or in jail for a long time. I understood beef and felt that it was necessary at times. I told them, "If you niggas can find a solution, then find it, so niggas can get back to the money." I had love for all of these niggas. I wanted to see them all prosper more than anything. No one listened.

Christine and I had been spending more and more time together. She was actually good peoples. She had two kids by some dude who didn't see them much and she had her own spot up north. She worked and took care of her kids without any help from their dad. I found that to be a trait of a strong, independent woman. She was nothing like my son's mom, Alicia. Alicia wasn't doing too well, although, she claimed to be living the life. She was still staying with her cousin Tamika and neither one of them were up to anything positive. I heard that Alicia was sleeping around which wasn't in her character. I guess after being in a relationship with me for three years, she felt it was time to spread her wings and vagina? However, that was none of my concern. I had plans to get my son but I couldn't do it until I got my shit together. I made a vow to myself to raise my son. I wasn't planning on going back to jail and I wanted to give my son everything that I could. There was no way in hell that I was going to be a "weekend" parent!

I had a daily routine. I would get up in the morning and head to an AA or NA meeting before I went to my drug and alcohol classes. I had to do outpatient treatment two days a week for about six months in order to get my driver's license back and to stay in compliance with D.O.C. I was cool with it. I got something out of it as far as motivation for the day. After that, I would go to the library and spend about an hour or two searching for jobs online, or I would go around and turn in some applications. I would go to grind and hustle for a little bit or run around and make some joogs off of my cell phone. I had a few different places that I would go at night. Most of the time, I would just go to my mom's house. It wasn't the safest place for my sobriety, but it was a spot where I could still make some joogs and get some money until I fell asleep. I was only selling weed because it's easier and less risky than selling any narcotic. I mean, I would "middle man" some coke deals if I could make a few bucks off the top. But I wasn't walking around with a sack anymore. With my record, a simple possession of cocaine would easily get me 3-5 years. I didn't want to risk that. At night, I would go to Christine's house if I didn't go to my mom's. She would drive from the north end and get me at any time of the night. I liked chilling with her. I would grab Lil Ty on Thursdays after attending my outpatient group and keep him for the weekend. I hesitated taking him to Christine's house in the beginning because I wanted to make sure it was real. I wasn't about bringing different women in and out of his life while I was looking for *the one*. He didn't need to see that. I wanted him to see me striving towards stability; not grossly misbehaving and using women. I was raising a man.

    I decided to give love a chance. It didn't take long for me to realize that Christine was legit. Most of the chicks that liked me, just liked "TLEE" or "Ty-Budd". They just liked *what* I was instead of *who* I was, and I understood that. Most of them wanted a dude who was about something. Simply having *potential* wasn't good enough. Christine loved Tyrome. She loved the fact that I had dreams and ambition. We were at the same points in our lives and wanted something different. She even supported my sobriety even though she wasn't in recovery. It had been a long time since I had a female who truly cared about me. However, it was the first time that I had a real woman in my life, as well.

    Christine had a son named Jo-Jo who was exactly the same age as Lil Ty. She also had a daughter, Octavia, who was a year older than the both of them. They all got along well. However, Jo-Jo and Octavia were a little bit sharper than Ty because Christine had them in a daycare that was teaching them different things. Ty was a hood kid, who talked with a little slang, and was a little tougher. The kids argued because they were kids and that's just what kids do. But all in all, they gelled really cool together. After a while, I could envision us as a family. I never thought of myself as a family man because of my lifestyle. I didn't think this way even when I was with Alicia. I've always felt like I would end up in prison because of all of the shit I did. I've always thought that I'd be some type of player or a rolling stone. Whenever I went to Christine's house, she would cook dinner, read to the kids, watch movies with them, we would go to parks, and all types of other domestic shit. I loved it!

Since I was spending more time at Christine's house, I ended up finding a part-time job out north at a glass factory. The owner of the company was also my new weed connect. He was cool and agreed to hire me to keep D.O.C. off my ass. I didn't have to be there all the time. I just needed him to let the D.O.C. know that I had a job. His name was Greg. He had a direct streamline with some Canadian smugglers. He didn't move much weed until he met me. I mean…he slung a few pounds here and there to a couple of people that he knew. But once I told him that I could move his whole shipment in one or two days, he got me in contact with his people. They never dealt with people in the Seattle area because they were known to be grimy and cutthroat. But knowing me served to be a great asset to them. Once I let Tyree know about my new connect and how much cheaper we could get the weed, he and his crew bit and we started making money. The good thing was that I was making money and I didn't have to do much. Greg would bring me five pounds at $2,500 a piece. Around this time, weed was going for around $3,200 a pound in the town. It could go for higher if you could find better quality weed. I'd take one pound for myself. Tyree would move the others and split the profit with me. Then, we would give Greg his $12,500. After about a month of doing things this way, they started bringing us 10-15 pounds at a time, and we started making more money. The more weed we got, the cheaper they'd charge us because we were moving it so fast. We would lower the prices in the streets to show some love in the hood. If it got better for us, then it got better for the streets. This was a good time to be making money. But there was still a war going on though...

    I remember watching the news one morning and seeing that the homie Big T-Kid was murdered and found dead near Seward Park. The news footage showed him outside of a Seattle nightclub as he was hitting a Seahawks player in the head with a pole, seriously injuring him. The Seahawks player was originally from Tacoma and had ties to the Crips out there. Investigators found it mysterious that T-Kid was found dead the morning after assaulting the football player. It was weird, but they had it entirely wrong. I knew T-Kid and was cool with him. I kicked it with him a few times when I was younger and he looked out me for in the joint when I did my first stretch. As far as I was concerned, he was a cool cat. Obviously, someone else felt differently about him. The Tacoma connection ended up being a false lead. The OG's from Deuce 8 communicated with some Tacoma factors and got assurance that no one from

Tacoma had anything to do with T-Kid's murder. T-Kid was a well-respected G and one of the founding members of Deuce 8. The OG's made it very clear that there would be retaliation for his death. The OG's were upset and did their own investigation to find out what happened to T-Kid. They didn't start questioning cats until after his funeral. They wanted to wait so that they could see which well-known G's didn't show up to the funeral. Questions and speculations started circulating around town but there were way too many rumors to determine the truth. People started making implications, which led to more rumors being spread, and more hostility arising in the hood.

Tyree and I heard from our sister Takari a couple of times but it was just a few phone calls and text messages. We thought she lived out of state. But we found out that she had been in Washington State for years, living with her grandmother. As a matter of fact, she lived in Tacoma; which was about 45 minutes south of Seattle. We arranged a time and place to meet up and reunite.

We met up on a Saturday afternoon. Tyree and I brought our sons with us because she wanted to meet her nephews, too. Takari was beautiful and looked just like our Auntie Vernice. She still resembled her baby photos but had grown into a beautiful young lady! We were all happy to see her and we greeted each other with hugs and tears of happiness. We sat back and talked for a while. We missed out on a lot of Takari's life and so did our dad. We wanted to know how things were going in her life and to tell her about ours. We were sure that her mother told her stories about our family that weren't too pleasant.

Takari's mother, Jackie, married a man named Doug after my dad went to prison. He was a basketball player who played for the Sacramento Kings at the time. We figured they were more than likely living the good life since he was doing well in the league. Takari told us that she had been living with her grandma in Washington for quite some time now, while her mother and stepfather lived in California. Her mom and Doug had two other children that lived with them in California. I didn't understand why she didn't live with them, but soon it became clear.

You see…Jackie was brown-skinned and Doug was mixed with Black and White. That means that the children they had together were also light-skinned. Takari was dark; just like the rest of us Lees. I'm guessing that it didn't look right to have a fair-skinned couple with two fair-skinned kids and a dark one? That alone, probably made her feel like the black sheep. The family photos would call for speculation and eventually lead to questions. Shortly after the questions, the issue of Takari's birth father would've come up. I'm sure that Jackie didn't want anyone digging too far into her past or finding out that she was once married to a convicted drug dealer. To prevent any of this from happening, she just sent Takari to live with her mother in Washington and never thought twice about it.

One would've thought that with the money Doug was making playing professional basketball, Jackie would've made sure that Takari and her grandma were well taken care of. Takari told us that they were actually struggling. She said that she had a lot of resentment against her mother for sending her away while the rest of the family lived the good life in California. She knew that it was because of her skin color and nothing else. This resulted in her feeling insecure during her childhood. She told us that her insecurity led to depression, and that depression led to her isolating herself. Jackie made sure that Takari had no contact with our side of the family. She didn't want us to know how she was treating my dad's daughter because we would have more than likely done something about it. I didn't understand the vile acts of Takari's mother or why she would keep her from a family that would have shown her nothing but love!

We couldn't repair the past or do anything to heal the wounds that her mother made on her heart. We just let her know that we were her brothers and that we were here for her now. We got her in contact with our dad because we were sure that they had a lot of catching up to do, too. Dad lost contact with Jackie and Takari back in 1993. Dad always claimed that Jackie played a part in him being busted in 1990. He said that his drug connections in California were actually her people and that she introduced him to them. He also said that she tried to broker a deal between him and her people in 1993, but he never did any business with them. Later, he found out that they were actually informants working for the feds.

"Being reconnected with our loved ones can be one of the greatest experiences felt. It gives us an opportunity to share memories, restore feelings, and resolve any friction made through absence. You begin to appreciate each other for the significant role one plays in your life. But, we have a lot of questions..."

Reconciliation

It had been almost a decade since I talked to my dad. I heard that he was having a hard time in prison and was moved to one of the more dangerous maximum-security facilities within the federal prison system. Tyree started communicating with him while I was locked up and I started talking to him a little after being released. We had a lot of catching up to do. Tyree, Uncle Tommy, and I arranged a trip to visit him but it got stalled due to my active D.O.C. status. Apparently, I had to have a hearing and show just cause for me to visit an inmate in the Federal Bureau of Prisons. I thought that this should have been simple; he was my dad and I hadn't seen him in years. My uncle explained the difficulties in dealing with that faction of the system and advised me to get an attorney for the hearing. Tyree had a homeboy named Zack from middle school who had just passed the bar exam. Zack and Tyree kept in touch over the years and were still pretty close. He was on his way to becoming an appellate lawyer and agreed to appear at the hearing and represent me for next to nothing. After the hearing, I was allowed to visit my dad. A week later, we boarded a plane and headed to the United States Penitentiary in Leavenworth, Kansas.

Seeing our dad was amazing! I've never realized how much I looked just like this dude! Tyree and I were both taller than him now. He was proud, surprised, and amazed at how big his boys had grown. I couldn't explain the feelings that I felt while seeing my dad for the first time in over 10 years. Tyree and my dad had grown closer while I was locked up. We all sat there and chopped it up for hours about the old and the new.

Pops was scheduled to be release in about three more years and we discussed what we were going to do. We talked about our boys and the women that we had in our lives. He also wanted to know how our mom was doing. Pops asked everything that he could on the first visiting day. He knew that we were going to be there two more times before we headed back home to Seattle, but he kept the conversation coming. The first day was filled with joy and happiness. We didn't want the visit to end. Good thing we were coming back the next day.

The second day mostly consisted of family issues and the horrors that he'd been dealing with while in prison. Pops told us that things went bad after he welched on the deal with the Feds in '93. They placed him in a maximum-security prison with bad paperwork. You see...first, you have to understand the politics of federal prison. There were gangs in the federal prison system. There were your Crips, Bloods, GD's, etc. If you weren't part of a gang, then you probably ran with a certain clique like the Muslims, Skinheads, Mexicans, or some other organization that had numbers. If that wasn't the case either, you could always run with people from the same city or state you came from. These cliques or gangs were called "cars"; meaning you rode with them. The problem was that Pops wasn't a gang member or a Muslim. There wasn't a Seattle or Washington State car due to their low numbers in the prison system. If there were someone from Seattle or

Washington, they would usually ride with one of the other cars. If an individual wanted to communicate or participate with any dealings of the cars, the shot callers would wanna check the individual's paperwork. Dad's paperwork indicated he worked with the Feds. It didn't say that he snitched on anyone (because he didn't), but it implicated that he agreed to work with the Feds. The very mentioning of that made things very difficult for him to function within a maximum-security prison. You couldn't do anything in these prisons without presenting your paperwork to the shot callers first. You couldn't bet, go to certain parts of the yard, or go into the TV room because certain cars had rights to or ran these places and activities. Sometimes you couldn't even sit down in the chow hall because cars owned the tables. Even if people hadn't read his paperwork, they still heard about it from other members. Pops was basically labeled as a snitch. This made people who weren't even riding with any particular car, not affiliate with him. Many different cars targeted him because of his faulty paperwork. Pops said that he was jumped and beaten by different crews due to him not bowing down or letting them extort him. He said that he asked his sister, Auntie Vernice, for help on numerous occasions, but to no avail. Vernice knew the ins and outs of making and designing paperwork. At one point, he just got rid of the paperwork and sent it to Vernice for her to alter but he hadn't received anything from her in years.

Pops said that he'd been to hell and back since being transferred to maximum-security. He was more hurt than upset because he did everything for the family when he was out. He bought cars, houses, and jewelry for everyone, and even took a deal that consisted of the Feds not prosecuting their mother and allowing them to keep the house. He felt betrayed and felt resentment towards his mother for allowing Vernice to neglect fixing his paperwork. They were still living in the house that he bought. He didn't blame Uncle Tommy as much because he knew that he had been in and out of prison himself for the last 20 years. He knew that Uncle Jerome made some effort to make sure he was cool and paid the Crip shot callers to protect him when he was locked up in Colorado. He did this because he thought Vernice was still getting the paperwork ready. Uncle Jerome was currently doing time in prison for the murder that his son Jay was convicted of, so he was out of commission. Whatever the case, Pops was going through hell and felt betrayed by his mother and sister.

After the visit, we went back to the hotel with a whole new perspective of the family. We questioned Uncle Tommy on what he knew about what Pops said and he appeared clueless. We've always had the upmost respect and love for our aunt and especially, our grandma. We couldn't even imagine them intentionally putting our dad in harm's way. This baffled my brother and I, but we both understood there had to be more to the story.

The third day was cool. We sat back and joked around for a majority of the time. Pops told us about what he heard was going on in the hood and asked about T-Kid's murder. I was surprised that he asked us about that. But, I also wondered why that particular question came up? I honestly didn't know anything about it. But when he asked, he was specifically looking at Tyree. Tyree looked puzzled himself and said, "Shit, I don't know!" Pops said, "I heard you got a little crew out there and you guys have been putting in work. Word is that someone from your crew might've had something to do with that shit." Tyree denied knowing anything about it. Pops heard a lot of things about what was going on in the hood and this was his first time asking anyone face-to-face regarding the validity of it. Prison chatter spreads just as fast as street rumors. Sometimes it spreads even faster because it has less space to travel.

Pops gave my brother and I some advice before we left. He advised Tyree to simmer down the beef in the hood and to try to be safe. He knew that there were probably a few dudes out there who might've had it in for him. He told me to keep my ass out of jail and to make sure my little brother was safe. Tyree was much bigger than most and his size frightened people at times. But Pops knew that I was the big brother and that Tyree listened to and respected me, more than any other man.

Tyree snuck some weed in and Pops was able to hide it in his ponytail during the visit. As we left, we all hugged one more time and we told him that we would be back soon. We left and headed to the airport. We were on the plane when I decided to ask Tyree about the T-Kid mess. I said, "Why didn't you tell me that people were implicating your homeboys?" He said, "Because I was waiting for shit to die down like the rest of the rumors." I said, "Ok, so now that it's reached all the way to fucking Leavenworth, you wanna let your big bro know what the hell is going on?" Tyree told me that T-Kid was supposed to meet him at his spot that night. He said that T-Kid called him and said that he had some exclusive weed that he got from someone and that he could have it at a really good price. Tyree said that he was there for hours waiting on him but he never came through. He must've decided to go clubbing first before he came through? Whatever the case, Tyree said that he left the spot, but heard that T-Kid might've stopped by after he was gone. He didn't tell me who was at the house when he left because he didn't want me to think that any of his boys had anything to do with it. I knew that he wasn't telling me the whole truth but I accepted it for the time being. Later, I learned that Mello and two other guys were at the house when he left. I didn't bother trying to figure out who the other two guys were, who was involved, or what circumstances had taken place.

"You have no fucking idea what beef is. After a certain point you forget how it started, who's all involved, or how to end it. You can easily get involved by simply hanging with the wrong people or being in the wrong place at the wrong time. Sometimes, we can be in beef with people and not even know it until it's too late. We also inherit the beefs. The Hatfield's and the McCoy's feuded for nearly two centuries and most of the participants, from both sides, don't have a clue as to what or who started the feud."

Family Ties Broken

We got back to town and things still weren't going very well in the hood. Mello got into some trouble and was booked. Apparently, Mello was arrested for a drive by shooting and was facing a couple of years in prison. He bailed out and continued his carnage against his enemies. Dank was still in prison for a shootout that he took part in outside of a club after he beat some dude up. He'd been down for some time and missed the LP-Union/Deuce 8 beef and the after effects of T-Kid's murder. Dank was cool with T-Kid but he didn't know any of the details behind the murder, either. He knew that Tyree wasn't involved and that all of the implications were false. Dank was the one giving us information on what was being said about T-Kid's murder through prison chatter.

Even with the main players booked, the beef was still going on. Soon, it became a senseless beef and people were committing senseless acts of violence. A few people got shot during a short amount of time and the ensuing violence were mainly due to retaliation of each other's previous actions. However, the LP's were in the middle of the beef. They were still beefing with the Union cats behind Def shooting Mello, but they were both locked up. Whatever the case, rumors started spreading and some people were making implications about certain LP members and their possible involvement in Big T-Kid's murder. It wasn't long before Deuce 8 started their spout with the LP's too. Deuce 8 and Union had a long history of comradery in the streets, as well as, inside of prison. So, the two of them cliquing together against the LP's seemed all too eminent. It wouldn't have to be a shot-caller's decision because the beef trickled down to a rift between street soldiers. The LP's were just a mere portion of their counterparts but they still proved to be resilient. Douggie took the reins.

Flames had three younger brothers but Douggie was the most talented when it came to street smarts. Yeah, he was having money with the bank licks, but Douggie was known more for putting in work against other crews when they were making their bones hanging paper. He was cool with members from the other gangs before the beefs started. He never resorted to claiming any specific set or being a part of a gang because he considered himself as a trendsetter. Douggie and his two older brothers decided to start a crew of their own, Low Profile, LP. When the beef started, he was the one putting in the most of the work and calling the shots. He was shot by a dude named "Squeeze" from Union while he was coming out of his momma's house one day, and he went on a rampage. He got hit in the shoulder and another bullet grazed his head. Squeeze thought that he killed him and drove off, but Douggie got up and gave chase. They had a shootout that lasted for over a mile! They damn near tore the hood up. They were speeding and shooting up and down residential streets! Douggie was pissed that someone shot him in front of his mom's house. He felt like it was a major ethical violation amongst gangsters. Once he realized that there were no rules, he single-handedly gave the Union cats the business for about a week straight! He became one of the main reasons why the beef intensified. Douggie was purely a savage and had more heart than any man twice his size. Indeed, he was a person that you would rather have as a friend than an enemy. He put in work and had love for those close to him.

Douggie had a high level of love and respect for Tyree and my brother Thomas. When Douggie was a youngster, Tyree always looked out for him. Tyree took Douggie under his wing long before he began breaking bread with his older brothers. When Douggie was younger, he was being bullied by some older guys in the neighborhood and told Tyree about it. Immediately, Tyree put a stop to it and told everyone that if they fucked with Douggie, then they would have a problem with him. Douggie loved him for that. Thomas and Douggie were the same age and went to elementary school together. They were very good friends while growing up. The got into a lot of trouble together when they were younger and always had each other's back. Once they got older and hit the block, Tyree showed Thomas and Douggie the ins and outs and provided them with the game they needed; like a big brother/big homie should. Douggie knew that Tyree was a standup dude and that Thomas' loyalty was like no other. He displayed loyalty towards them. Even though they ran with different cliques, they always kept each other in the loop.

Rumorville was working hard on the T-Kid murder. But this time, the rumors linked the LP's and my brother's crew to the murder. Whenever someone asked or confronted Mello about it, it would almost always end up in gunfire. He didn't like being implicated. The case was cold but the cops had possible suspects. One day, I went to see my D.O.C. officer and Detective Cobain was there. I knew that this was more than odd because my D.O.C. officer was located in West Seattle and Cobain worked the East Precinct. I hadn't done any dirt in a while and wasn't packing anything either, thankfully. Obviously, Cobain had been talking to my D.O.C. officer before I arrived. I could tell by the look that she gave me when I came into her office. Cobain said, "What's up, Mr. Lee?" I didn't respond. I wanted to know why he was there. I figured that his presence would mean that my D.O.C. officer might question my compliance. However, I was in good standing. I hadn't been violated in over a year. I had a job, gave clean piss, and was making timely payments towards my restitution. Cobain said, "I guess you're wondering why I'm here? Well, I'm searching for answers regarding T-Kid's murder. I don't think you did it but I know that you know who did." I told him, "I don't know shit." Then I asked, "And what did you tell her?" Cobain said, "I didn't tell her anything that she doesn't already know. I just got here five minutes ago so there hasn't been much of a discussion." I gave him the "bullshit" face. He continued, "Look T, I could've pulled you over in the hood and brought you down to the station or came to your house. But I met you here so that others wouldn't know. Now, I know you play advice council to your little brother's crew and that you know something. How about you tell me what I need to know and I'll make sure nothing comes back to you and your brother? I know that T-Kid came to your brother's house that night but your brother had already left. I know that Mello was there and I'm close to finding out who was there with him." It was a known fact that Cobain didn't like Mello. He would always find a way to elude Cobain whenever he tried to approach him. Cobain hated running so he hated the people that ran from him. I said, "Shit, well you know way more than I know. I'm a family man now. You're barking up the wrong tree." Then he pleaded, "Come on T, this is your chance to help stop a lot of the violence that has been going on in the hood." I honestly didn't know what he wanted me to say. I guess he wanted me to implicate someone, or say that I heard or knew something that he didn't know? I wasn't even playing dumb because I really didn't know. But if I did know, I wouldn't have told him shit!

 I listened as Cobain continued to fish for information, but it was time for me to leave. I said, "Well Detective, good luck with your investigation and I'm sorry that I can't help you out. But I don't know anything and I haven't heard any rumors. Now, Ms. Crawford, can I take this piss test so that I can leave? I gotta get ready for work soon." Cobain ended with, "Look T, I know that you know what happened. And I know that your brother does too. If I find out that you're holding back, I'm going to arrest you and charge you with obstruction. When I arrest Mello for the murder, I'm going to find a way to charge your brother with accessory after the fact." I told him, "Good luck with that too." Then I left.

As time passed, things started to shift in our lives. We were focused on helping our dad figure out what he wanted to do once he got out of prison. Tyree's patnas, Dank and Mello, were still in prison on gun charges so he was still in slow motion. I still had my weed connect poppin but it was on a smaller scale. My main concern was keeping Tyree out of the hood. There was a lot of talk going around the hood stemming from T-Kid's murder and I didn't want him getting caught up in that mess. We were having long talks about transitioning out of the game and going completely legal. We envisioned the real estate game as a profitable means or opening up some kind of business or a nightclub. We were hustlers at heart and that couldn't be denied. We loved our homies, the street life, and what it represented. But we didn't like taking penitentiary chances to provide for our families. As much as we loved our dad, we didn't want to end up like him. We were hell-bent on raising our kids.

Tyree had a spot up north for a little bit. Neka got a job with the city that paid well, so Tyree mainly stayed home with the kids and made joogs out that way. I liked it because it kept him out of harm's way. My intentions were to always protect him in any way that I could. There were times in our lives when Tyree and I were at odds, but it never came to blows. Protecting him never resulted in bullying him or using force. He was a big little brother. I made a lot of mistakes that he learned from and I learned from some of his, too. He had homies that would always ride for him, but I was the only one who would *die* protecting him.

Grandma had been living in the house that Dad bought but it was literally falling apart and needed major work. This house was the only piece of property that the Feds let my dad keep, because it wasn't in anyone's name that was mentioned in the original indictment in 1990. Grandma had been living in it for the last fifteen years. Essentially, it served as a safe haven for us whenever we were in a bind or when someone got out of jail or prison and needed somewhere to stay while they got their shit together. The house was in my dad's brother, Uncle Shelton's, name. The money that Grandma was getting from her monthly checks weren't enough to cover the existing mortgage, insurance, property taxes, and other bills that needed to be paid. Uncle Shelton lived in North Carolina, so Aunt Vernice was the only one around to take care of Grandma around the clock. Vernice had her own issues with raising a family of her own. She had legal troubles and was supporting her own unknown inflictions. The condition of the house had gotten so bad that Grandma couldn't live in it anymore. She ended up moving in with Aunt Vernice.

Tyree was in the housing loop with his family over the last two years. He always had a trap spot but he kept a clean spot for his family. He started franchising his weed game to other parts of the country and had some peeps down in ATL that he got down with. They developed a plan to transport weed from Seattle to Atlanta to sell it at a significantly higher price. I was the one shipping it but the plan flopped a few times because of the high demand. It would usually touch down but heat followed whenever it didn't land. Tyree had to get it out of there before the people who were getting knocked revealed his name. After a few runs, he eventually came home and stayed.

With the big house falling apart, we developed a plan to sell it and get some money so that Dad could start over. No one else was concerned about the status of the house. Everyone moved out, moved on, or completely ignored the needs of the house. We talked to Uncle Shelton and he told us that the money we got from selling the house in Seattle could possibly buy two or three houses in North Carolina. We bit. Uncle Tommy and Uncle Jerome were both locked up and Vernice wasn't putting any money into repairing the house, so we figured that selling it was the best thing to do. Vernice was highly upset and opposed everything about it. She never took the time to fully listen to the plans that we had. Plus, she didn't even live in the house anymore, anyway. Shit, the house was in such bad shape that even Grandma wasn't living in there anymore. They weren't paying the mortgage, putting money towards repairs, or had any intentions of dealing with it at all. It was just rotting away!

Tyree had a killer idea that had significance to our family in the future. Neka's dad, Richard, had been in the real estate business for years. He bought and sold houses but he also rebuilt and remodeled them too. Richard and Tyree both knew what the big house was worth and that it would be profitable for it to be on the market. Richard figured that if the house went on the market that it could sell for as much as $750,000. He figured this based on the size of the land and the potential of building more properties on it. I did my own research with Uncle Shelton and found out that if we invested $100,000 into the house and the land, that we could possibly clear a mill! But we didn't have a $100,000, we didn't know how long it would take to make the repairs/additions, or what kind of bullshit would transpire during that time. Tyree brokered a deal between Richard and Uncle Shelton to sell the property *as is* for $700,000. It was less than our projections but it took care of certain issues. It was enough to pay the rest of the mortgage off and still have enough money left over to do more real estate investing once my dad got out of prison. Richard granted us three things by way of this deal being sealed. First, he agreed to let Tyree live in the house rent-free until our dad got out. This was so that Tyree could do some repairs and to keep anything else from being damaged. Secondly, Richard allowed us to keep all of Dad's cars on the land until he came home and had the means to remove them. The last deal that was granted to us was an unspoken one. Tyree was selling the house to his son's grandfather, who was also Richard's only grandson at the time. This nearly guaranteed that the house would eventually end up in the Lee name again in the future.

Selling the house started an inner family feud between Aunt Vernice and us. She felt that it wasn't up to us to sell the house and that she should've received a majority of the profit from the sale. There was no way that she was going to get any money out of Tyree, Shelton, or I! In all actuality, it was still Dad's house! He was the one who bought the house. Of course, Dad had plans to take care of his people when he came home. Dad offered her and Grandma $25,000 to make things right for the family until he came home. She refused to take anything and even tried to stop the deal. On several occasions, Aunt Vernice tried to sabotage my brother's life for doing what his uncle and father instructed him to do. If Tyree felt like what he was doing was wrong, I'm sure that he wouldn't have done it. But he had to take a serious look at where Dad and Uncle Shelton were coming from. Pops was basically in prison and left for dead by those who he cared about the most. When he flourished, he made sure the whole family shined! Even when the heat came down, he showed his loyalty by taking pleas on the contingency of charges being dropped on other family members, including Grandma and Vernice. His original deal with the Feds also made it possible to keep the house even though the government claimed it was bought with drug money. He did all of this for them and was hung out to dry! In all actuality, that house was his and they knew it! They had all of the resources, time, and opportunities to use the equity in the house to expand and build with, but never utilized it as an asset. They just used it as a spot to stash Grandma Maureen and as a sanctuary for people to stay at when they were in a jam.

Uncle Shelton had different reasons for selling the house. It had been in his name for over 10 years. He took it under his wing the last time that he lived in Seattle. At one point, the house was on the list for foreclosure due to unpaid taxes. He paid off a bunch of the taxes and put the house in his name so that he could refinance it and make the major repairs that were needed. He moved in with Grandma while he was doing the repairs and was paying the mortgage while he stayed there. Once he left, he told Grandma and Vernice to pay the mortgage and taxes however they could. Back then, Vernice and her husband were making money hustlin' and Grandma received money from Social Security and other sources. They kept up the house for a couple of years, but then, for some reason, they stopped paying the full mortgage and taxes. This meant that Shelton had to pay whatever portion they didn't pay out of his own pocket. There were times in which they didn't pay anything *at all* towards the mortgage. Then Uncle Shelton would have to cover it himself. This bothered Shelton because he was adamant about keeping his credit in good standing and he had his own family to take care of. He could've easily said "fuck the house" and allowed it to get foreclosed, but it would have had a negative affect on his credit. He wanted out. A while back, he offered to give me the house but I declined because I didn't know much about the real estate game and I was still bangin' and pushin'. So when Tyree, my dad, and I came to him about selling the house, he jumped on it. He wanted nothing more than to get the house sold, and out of his name, so that he could move on with his own ventures. I guess tending to the house was holding him back? I think he may have had ulterior motives but I didn't blame him at the time.

The ordeal with the house intensified when Vernice's efforts to stop the deal went sour. She tried to hire a lawyer but each one told her that she didn't have a viable case. The fact of the matter was that the house wasn't hers or Grandma's. Legally, it belonged to Shelton because his name was the only name on the deed. After all of her failed attempts, she decided to sabotage the property and started tearing the house apart! She started breaking the windows on the house and on the cars parked in the driveway! Tyree wanted to put hands on her because Neka and his son were in the house when she was breaking shit. Tyree had a high level of respect for our aunt and he pleaded with her to stop. He could've easily done plenty of things to physically restrain her but the fact that she was his aunt prevented that. She did such an extensive amount of damage to the house. Tyree, Neka, and their son had to move out due to the amount of damage she made. Richard, the new owner of the house, stepped in. He was going to have charges pressed against Vernice but Tyree begged him not to. Tyree said, "Hey Rich, the house is insured plus I know you're gonna be doing some demolition work on it anyway. She's actually helping. Let her think that she's doing something." He didn't call the cops but he moved Tyree and his family out and had the house locked, boarded up, and put a security fence around it so that she couldn't do any further damages. He let Tyree and his family move into one of his houses in the CD until they found another spot. I hated this for a number of reasons. The main reason was due to all of the shit that was going on in the CD. Little did Aunt Vernice know…she put my brother back into harm's way.

There was still a strong residue of Mello and Def's beef lingering in the streets. Plus, people were still implicating Tyree's crew and the LP's of being connected to T-Kid's murder. Dank was still locked up but was due to be released soon. He was Tyree's right-hand man. Douggie got shot and survived, but was doing time behind check cashing schemes. Flames was locked up too. Somehow, he managed to get himself caught up in a shootout with some dudes that were implicating him and his brothers in some shady shit. He surprised niggas when he decided to try to lay his murder game down! I knew that I couldn't protect my brother from everything but I looked out for him the best that I could. The truth is…Tyree was a street soldier first. Yeah, he was a leader and led a strong crew. But he also went to war with them and stood on the front line; just like the

Greek Warrior - King Leonidas. This guy had *mad love* for the hood and was never going to desert it because of some beef that somebody had with him, or his homeboys. He felt like the hood belonged to him and that he belonged to the hood.

"How do I process the indefinite case of mortality? Can I question God for His actions? At some point, my only plans are to make others feel the same pain that I've experienced. My gut-wrenching pains demoralize my character, which causes me to display malicious intentions, and to do so in front of those that I have the deepest respect for. Please be worried by the actions, for I am no longer in control."

Just When Things Started to Improve…

I had a run in with T-Kid's younger brother Trevor. I saw him at the corner store one day. I was walking in as he was walking out. We caught eye contact with one another and I said, "What's up nigga?" in a very semi-aggressive tone because I didn't like the way that he was looking at me. I heard that he was running around talking shit after his brother got killed. We never considered him as a threat unless he had a gun in his hand and all ten of his fingers were working properly. He was on the local news implying that some Tacoma dudes had something to do with T-Kid's death. I knew that he was hurt but niggas acted like he wasn't "dry-snitchin" on TV.

Trevor replied and said, "Yeah, you niggas think shit is over?" I said, "Whachu talking about?" as I stepped closer to him. Now…I admit…a few years earlier, I might've thought twice before stepping to him because I was much smaller back then. But now, I was looking down to him and he didn't want it. Trevor said, "You niggas know what happened to my brother and that shit ain't cool!" I told his ass, "I don't know what happened to your brother! But I know you ain't implicating me?! And who is "you niggas"? He just walked away and looked at me like he had something planned. I didn't trust him. I followed him as he started to get into his car. I grabbed him and threw him to the ground. I thought he was going for a gun. He said "Man, whachu doin?!" I didn't say anything. I thought about stomping him out and beating the shit out of him. But, I didn't. I just stood over him asserting my dominance. I asserted my dominance over him as a reminder that if he was gonna come at me, he had better come correct! I had my gun on my waist and he saw it. I didn't pull it out because I didn't need to. I stepped over him and walked away.

    I've known Trevor for a little bit longer than I've known his brother. We attended the same middle school but I didn't really get along with him. I mean…we never had any beef or anything. I just didn't like him. He was a little bit older than me and more popular back then. I thought Trevor was arrogant, pompous, and was only known for being T-Kid's younger brother. One time, he tried to pick on me at school and quickly found out that shit wasn't going to work on me! This dude hadn't put in any work or made a name for himself. The big homies looked out for him just because he was T-Kid's little brother, which was cool, but that was his only claim to fame. Everything he did or received was because he was T-Kid's little brother. This guy was Tito Jackson. I mean…people knew that I was Tyrome Lee's son, but that was only amongst the older crowd. My peers knew me as TLEE or Ty-Budd. Most of them didn't even know who my dad was. I had respect for T-Kid. He was a G to me. He was a trendsetter, a founding member of Deuce 8, and niggas respected him for being real to the game. He was widely respected in the streets and in prisons. A lot of people called Trevor "Little T-Kid", but I didn't. I respected T-Kid. Trevor was a bitch to me, and it felt like I'd be disrespecting a real one by calling this dude "Little T-Kid".

Almost a year passed and Tyree had his daughter Tyra. Christine gave birth to our first daughter, Tyliyah, soon after. I took Alicia to court to get custody of Lil Ty and won. I already had primary custody of him for a year.

What happened was…one day I went to pick Ty up from his mom and simply said that he was coming to live with me. By this time, Christine and I were living together, I had a job, a car, a driver's license, and Alicia wasn't doing shit but living with her cousin and sitting on her ass. She disputed it for about a week or two, but there wasn't anything she could do. I got him into school, got him up to date with his immunizations, and put him into a family learning environment. I believed that Black boys needed to be raised by Black men; primarily, their fathers. I wasn't going to allow myself to be a weekend dad while she had various men around my son. Fuck that! Christine and I established a family, planned a future together, and Lil Ty was part of it. He went to visit Alicia on weekends.

But this was the fucked up part. Lil Ty had been living with me for about a year when I received a letter in the mail from the prosecuting attorney. It stated that I owed child support! I was confused.

When I looked deeper into it, I found out that the whole time Lil Ty had been living with me, Alicia was receiving welfare checks for him from the state. This had me pissed off something bad! I couldn't understand why she thought this was alright or if she thought I wasn't going to find out? I really wanted to hurt this bitch! I didn't know what to do or who to plead my case to.

I was too upset to call Alicia to confront her about it. I knew that if I did, I would end up calling her a bag of bitches! This would've led to her talking shit and a conundrum of other events. I called John and met up with him later that evening because I was belligerently upset. I started ranting, "Man, they gonna start garnishing my checks, suspend my license, and cause other financial woes for owing child support for a kid I take care of! Man, who does deceitful shit like this?" John listened to me ramble for a while then he asked, "Are you finished?" I said, "Whachu mean? Hell no! I ain't finished! I'm going to find a way to make her pay for this!" John had a smooth way of calming me down when I was upset like that. He wasn't a "Bible Thumper", but he frequently used quotes from it when necessary. One of his favorite quotes was, "A soft voice turns away wrath." When I was really upset, he would respond or give me advice in a very calm voice. John responded to rants about Alicia's actions by saying, "Man, calm down, T. The law is on your side. Now, I know that you got a couple of bucks saved up. Go get yourself a lawyer. You may have to spend a few bucks to make this right, but that's life. Acceptance is the key to your problems. You accept these problems first and then deal with them, accordingly. You can be upset at her actions as much as you want, but remember this: You chose her. Now deal with her, accordingly." His words didn't calm me down at that moment but after I left our meeting, I thought about it more.

I contacted a lawyer that John recommended. His name was Eric. He was this young Jewish dude, fresh out of law school, and he was hungry. Eric's dad and John were old high school buddies and they went way back. I met with him a week later. Eric specialized in Father's Rights and was shocked by what I was going through. I told him my situation, paid him, and watched him work. He got me the temporary custody order and put everything in motion for me to get full legal custody of my son. In the end, I was granted full custody and Alicia had to pay child support to me! It could've ended up a lot better for her if she had just signed over custody to me in the beginning, before trial. She refused and was being the stubborn person that she always was. Her stubbornness cost me nearly $5,000. But it was worth being named the legal custodial parent of Tyrome Lee, III. She still had visitation but she couldn't use him for any benefits, take him outside of the state without my permission, or use him as a pawn for leverage. The courts granted her visitation every other weekend but I sent him to her every weekend. I made sure that Ty had as much time with his mom as possible. But my lawyer told me to never allow him to go over to her house more than three days out of the week. She may have felt like I did this to spite her for her actions after we broke up, but I already moved on from that shit. My only concern was my son's well-being and not being punished for taking care of him.

I had a daughter. I was blessed and granted the opportunity by God to witness Christine give birth to my daughter. It was the most beautiful thing I had ever seen! I've seen childbirth before and was there when Lil Ty was born, but this was different. Lil Ty's birth was a C-section, so I missed out on nature's natural birth process. To watch *My Love* give birth to my child was something that I would always cherish! I owed her my world! I was in love with Christine at this point, but after watching her go through the painful event of giving birth to my daughter, it made my love for her grow a thousand times stronger! Tyliyah Lannett was the most beautiful thing I'd ever seen before in my life. I tell her that her every day, until this day! She had my thick eyebrows, big lips, and nose, with her mother's finesse. This was my baby alright! I swear that I held her for hours before I let anyone else hold her. This was MY BABY. I loved her more than anything in the world. I loved all my children equally, but this moment meant something different to me. This was a beautiful time for me.

I bought an old 1991 Caprice Classic from a car auction. It was an old police training vehicle and it had less than 75k miles on it. It ran good and just about everything was intact. I bought it in the wintertime and let it sit while I grabbed some pieces to make it shine. My patna BD sold me some 22-inch wire rims about 6 months before I even got the car. I didn't buy them with the intention of putting them on anything in particular. But he sold them so cheap that I couldn't refuse. I just put them in my garage until I found use for them. I had a patna that I grew up with named Amos. He'd been doing body and interior work on cars since we were kids. He opened up his own shop on the south side of Seattle and showed the homies love. Amos and I had history. We went to war with some Africans back in the day and nearly got killed by those crazy muthafuckas! We were able to shoot our way out of a jam and highjack a cab back to planet Earth. He didn't owe me any favors but we just always looked out for each other after that. The Caprice still had the "Training Vehicle" logo on the side of it when I took it to him. He gave me a deal on the interior work. He re-upholstered my seats and made them gun-metal gray, with a navy blue piping. He did the same to the interior roof, except he added a sunroof. He made the dashboards gray with a blue blend, inserted wood paneling, and restructured the placement of the stereo and climate controls. Next, he re-did the carpet flooring and stitched "TLEE" into the floors, and tinted the windows. I took the car home and let it chill for a couple of months before I took it to get painted.

    I bought a 350 rocket engine from the junkyard and had it put in. My little homie, Scarface, was a whiz at jacking beats from people and slanging them for the low. I don't know whose beats he sold me, but them shits were slappin! When summertime approached, I took that joint to the paint shop and had it painted glossy blue, candy-coated, with all types of flakes. I put the rims on after the paint job was done. Afterwards, I had the electronics installed. I had the stereo system installed and some TV screens put into the headrests. It was beautiful! I called it "The Hawk". You could hear me coming from miles away! If it wasn't the beats booming, then it was the roaring sound of my dual tailpipes rumbling. This was my stamp in the car game. I'd never tricked out a car before because my driver's license was always suspended. Usually, I'd just ride around in some kind of inconspicuous whip to get from point A to B. It was usually a cheap car that I could stand to lose because I never had a driver's license. But now that I had a driver's license and insurance, I went all out! I could invest $5,000 in a car without the fear of losing it. The Hawk had me stuntin' on cats.

The weed connect that we had from Canada, through Greg, had come to a stop. Greg had an experience that forced him to make a decision. He got set up and robbed by some people that were close to him. He was supplying some other cats with weed too, but eventually, they were unhappy with the amount of weed that he was able to supply them with. He gave most of the weed that came in to Tyree and I because we had the viable means to move it at a faster pace and we never tried to negotiate prices with him. Greg and I had a mutual friend named Kelsey who would usually cop 2-3 pounds out of the 10 that got through the border every two weeks. Before I came along, Kelsey could call Greg at any time and cop from him. But after I started copping from him, he was always out. After a while, Kelsey had to start copping from me. He didn't have a problem with me, but he constantly tried to talk down the prices because he knew, or had an idea, of what I was paying. I told him that I wasn't a middleman and if he wanted to pay Greg's prices, he would have to contact Greg. Whatever the case, it wouldn't make me or break me.

Kelsey and Greg had a disagreement that I knew nothing about. But it stemmed from me having first dibs on a majority of the supply that came in. Kelsey knew too much. He'd been dealing with Greg a lot longer than I had, and he knew a little more about his business and some of his connects. He even knew where Greg went to organize and gather the shipment after it crossed the border. He used this to his advantage and had him set up and robbed. Greg was no gangster but he wasn't a pussy either. When

Kelsey's people came to rob him, he actually put up a fight. Three armed men and one woman veered him off of the road after he left his stash spot, got him out of the car, and ran through his whip in broad daylight. He put hands on the broad and was giving one of the gunmen the business before another one of them shot him in the back. They fled off and left him on the side of the road bleeding before a passerby saw him and signaled for help. He didn't suffer any major life threatening injuries from the gunshot, but he had some minor scrapes and bruises from the fight that he put up. Greg was a little older and took this as a sign for him to leave the game. The robbers only made off with three and a half pounds but he felt like things could have been a lot worse. He said that he recognized one of the gunmen and that it was a dude that he had seen over at Kelsey's house before. He said he was sure of that. Tyree and I visited him in the hospital and told him that we would handle everything and make sure that Kelsey paid for his hand in this. Greg told us that he didn't want any retaliation. He said, "If you guys do something to him, that shit is gonna come back to me. I ain't trying to deal with that. Ain't no one coming to ask me questions and try to threaten me with any jail time for anything. I ain't no gangster. I'm out. So leave things be. I'll hook ya'll up with my connect and then you guys need to stay clear of me after that." This made us feel like he might reveal things that he knew about us if the heat came down on him. After our meeting with him, Tyree and I left. I told Tyree, "We're not fucking with him or anyone connected to him after that. Them cats are more cutthroat than niggas in the hood. Only difference is that they're upfront about it. If he's indicating he might tell, I'm sure whoever his connect is might be on the same shit." We didn't deal with Greg or any of his connects after that.

With our main connect gone the hood had dried up a little bit. I didn't know the weed we brought to the hood had such an impact on the streets. We mainly sold it in bulk; meaning nothing less than a quarter pound. It was a trip to realize how those joogs that we made trickled down and had a strong effect on the street-level market. We still had a few connects but a lot of them were leery of us because word had been spread around the town about all of the robberies that we did back in the day. We had a hard time finding it at a low enough price for us to slang it in bulk and still make a decent profit. If we couldn't find it that low, we would just have to break the weed down and make our money that way. But that meant more work. Sometimes when we couldn't find it for the price that we wanted or if we had to pay more, we could always make up the difference by sending it to one of our out-of-town connects. They always paid top dollar for Seattle weed because it was hard to find in most southern states. I had a knack for getting it there. We got a lot of love in places like ATL, Chicago, and spots up in Louisiana and Florida. We had a big homie named Black from Chicago that lived in Seattle. He was GD just like most of us up here. Whenever we sent weed that way, we'd hop on the next thing smoking and get it there. We got major love in the CHI.

Things in the hood had improved but there were plenty of visible, unresolved issues between hoods and blocks. I was at my mom's house one day chilling with her and Craig. They were doing pretty well. A lot of people's parents and families had been so broken by addiction that the problems and issues created were beyond repair. I think it was back in 1998, after Grandma Johnnie's passing, that my mom and Craig decided to get their lives together. Back then, Tyree and I were both almost about grown and out of the house, mostly. Thomas was around 12 years old and my youngest brother, CJ, was three years old. The absence of Tyree and I in the household played a part in them overcoming their addictions. Honestly, I never knew how bad it had gotten because they always kept things functioning. At least one of them always kept a job, so the bills were usually paid before shit got shut off. But you could tell what was going on by the company they kept.

My mom had a job in the YMCA's fundraising department and rose up in the ranks quickly. She had great organizational skills, a knack for interpreting clerical data, and displayed great leadership skills. Craig started doing volunteer work at a local foodbank before they hired him to run the facility. I loved the changes they made in their lives and it was inspiring! My younger brothers CJ and Thomas were the only ones living with them, but CJ was usually with me at my house. He was only five years older than Lil Ty and they were hella close. I started to take Tyliyah to my mom and Craig's house for a couple of hours every Sunday. I wanted my kids to have a close relationship with them more than anything. Lil Ty was already close to my mom, but I stressed the importance of my mom being close with Tyliyah, as well. My mom always wanted a daughter but ended up having four bad ass boys. Making sure that my daughter had a close relationship with my mom was the best that I could do for her. Plus, I was always fearful of my own mortality. I figured that if something happened to me, my kids would never have a problem adjusting to living with their grandparents, if needed. The relationship was already being established. I didn't know what the future had in store for me.

On the same day, I heard that there were two barbeques going on in the hood. There was one at Yesler Park being thrown by some of the homies from Deuce-8 and Deuce-0, and another one at Barnett Park that the homies from Union were throwing. I left my mom's house to head over there to see what was poppin. I had a few joogs over that way so I figured that I'd stop by and say what's up to some of my patnas. On my way there, my cousin Nikki called me and said that she heard someone was shot over by Barnett Park and that the medics were trying to revive them. I thought to myself, "Aw shit. This shit is still going on." I was already heading that way so I figured that I'd find out who it was and what happened when I got over there. I got another phone call less than a minute later from my brother Thomas. He screamed, "Ty, that was Tyree who got shot! I'm on my way over there now!" My heart dropped…